AMERICAN CAR SPOTTER'S GUIDE 1940-1965

REVISED EDITION

TAD BURNESS

Purchased at:
GRAND OLD CARS MUSEUM
201 W. Apache Trail
Apache Junction, Az. 85220
(602) 982-3500

Motorbooks International
Publishers & Wholesalers Inc.
Osceola, Wisconsin 54020, USA

©Tad Burness, 1978

ISBN: 0-87938-057-8
Library of Congress Catalog Card Number: 78-14879

All rights reserved. No part of this publication may be reproduced without prior written permission from the publisher; Motorbooks International Publishers & Wholesalers, Inc., P.O. Box 2, Osceola, Wisconsin 54020, U.S.A.

Printed in the United States of America

10 9 8 7 6 5 4 3

Library of Congress Cataloging in Publication Data
Burness, Tad, 1933-
  American car spotter's guide, 1940-1965.

  1. Automobiles—United States. 2. Automobiles—United States—Pictorial works. 3. Automobiles—United States—Identification. I. Title.
TL23.B78   1978   629.22'22'0973   78-14879
ISBN 0-87938-057-8

Introduction

This book is intended as a helpful tool. But first of all, it's for you to *enjoy!* Browsing leisurely through the pages is like a nostalgic 'time capsule' trip through the 1940's, 1950's and early 1960's.

They're all here, those fascinating, chrome-plastered, bright-colored American dreamboats from the jukebox era—all the four-wheeled friends you remember so well, plus many you may never have seen until now!

And you'll want to keep this collection around as a handy reference book and peaceful 'argument settler' when it comes to positively identifying one year model or make from another. All of the pictures are arranged alphabetically by make, and chronologically by year, with helpful notes on what identifying characteristics to watch for.

Some time ago this writer assembled a hand-made, personal 'car spotter' in a large scrapbook. It was bulky and crude compared to the book you have here, but any time it was carried along to car shows, club meetings, etc., others were anxious to borrow it and check out items of particular interest. "You really ought to make this into a book we could all buy," many suggested. There was a need for such a book, so I then prepared the original edition of the *American Car Spotter's Guide 1940-1965,* also published by Motorbooks International.

Since the publication of the old edition, many additional and much better pictures have been acquired, through the kindness of friends and through the purchase of hard-to-find ads, sales literature, etc. The time has at last come for this largely expanded, much improved and more complete edition. If you already own the former 213-page version, have no regrets—though this new book is more complete, the old one contains a few small pictures not used again, and therefore could remain of some interest for that reason.

Notice the many better pictures and close-up views in this new edition, as well as the additional written facts. Though this is a spotter's guide and not intended as an encyclopedia, there is helpful information concerning horsepower, wheelbase, tire size, original price, etc., of many of the cars shown here. Available space doesn't allow us to include all prices, specifications, and illustrations for all body types of every individual model in every case; because, then, this could become a 3,000-page, $150 thing the size of a Manhattan telephone directory that would weary you just to pick up! We're excited, though, about all the extra detail in this brand-new edition, and hope you're equally pleased.

You'll see many favorites here: the Kaisers and Frazers, the Studebakers, Hudsons, Packards, Fords and Mercurys, the durable Chrysler products and choice goodies such as the beautiful 'woodies'...and, of course, many beautiful Lincolns, Cadillacs, Buicks, the Chevies you love, and much, much more. This new edition even includes many rarities such as the fabulous '48 Tucker and others that did not get into full production but which have aroused your curiosity over the years!

Most cars were big and flashy in the era covered here. But if you like compacts and minicars, the Metropolitans and others are presented, plus many Crosley pictures not seen in the old edition.

Well, I could ramble on, but you're eager to get further into your new book and see the pictures. It's so easy to look up any car in which you're interested!

Concerning the prices included in some cases: they are f.o.b (freight on board) factory prices. In other words, they are the prices you would have paid had you taken delivery of the car at the factory, and without the added taxes, license and delivery fees. And then there were charges for various accessories or extras included. And prices were always subject to "change without notice," so that a new car might cost more than it had a few weeks or months previously.

Thank you for your interest! I'd certainly enjoy hearing from you if you have comments or suggestions about the book, and if you wish a personal reply, please enclose a self-addressed stamped envelope. And meanwhile, may this book be a handy tool you can use often.

Tad Burness
San Jose, Calif.

Acknowledgements

With deep gratitude to the following individuals, whose kind help in rounding up certain hard-to-find pictures or facts will always be appreciated! Bill Adams, Ronald C. Adams, David, Roger & John Allen, Jim Allen, Jeff Anderson, Bill Babich, Warren J. Baier, Larry Blodget, Jim Bollman, Paul Bridges, Edwill H. Brown, Emmett P. Burke, Swen H. Carlson, Steve Cifranic, John A. Conde, Virginia Daugert, Howard De Sart, Jim Edwards, Jim Evans, Fred K. Fox, Will Fox, Norm Frey, Jeff Gibson, Bruce Gilbert, Mark Gresser, Dick Grove, W. B. Hamlin, H. Gordon Hansen, Albert R. Hedges, Larry C. Holian, Corinne James, Alden Jewell, David Johnson, Elliott Kahn, Lenny Kellogg, John C. Kelly, Bruce Kennedy, Mark Kubancik, Mike Lamm, June Larson, Rick Markell, Keith Marvin, Larry Mauck, Carl Mendoza, Jim Miller, Harry Mosher, Bruce Newell, Dave Newell, Al Newman, Raymond B. Petersen, Tim Ressler, Walter F. Robinson, Lewis B. Scott, Jay Sherwin, Dave Sibert, Mark Simon, Kirk Slater, Craig Steele, John Stempel, Tom Terhune, R. A. Wawrzyniak, Paul Wehner, Kenneth Wilson, Bob Winke, and Robert Zimmerman.

Thanks are due, also, to the following corporations or associations for either making little-known facts public or for making direct contributions of pictures and/or information: American Motors Corp., Antique Automobile Club of America, Buick Club of America, Cadillac-La Salle Club, Chrysler Corp., Contemporary Historical Vehicle Assn. (CHVA), Corvair Society of America (CORSA), Crosley Automobile Club, De Soto Club of America, Edsel Owner's Club, Fabulous 50's Ford Club of America, Ford Motor Company, General Motors Corp. (& Divisions), Harrah's Automobile Collection, Hudson-Essex-Terraplane (HET) Club, International Edsel Club, Kaiser-Frazer Owner's Club (KFOC), Metropolitan Owner's Club, Milestone Car Society, Oldsmobile Club of America, Society of Automotive Historians, Studebaker Driver's Club, and the WPC/Chrysler Product Restorer's Club.

Table of Contents

Airway 7	Edsel 142	Metropolitan 228
American Bantam 7	Fairlane 145	Mustang (independent) 229
Beech Plainsman 7	Falcon 147	Mustang (Ford) 229
Bobbi Kar 7	Ford 150	Nash 231
Buick 8	Frazer 171	Olds F-85 239
Buick Special 28	Gordon Diamond 173	Oldsmobile 242
Cadillac 32	Graham (& Hupmobile) 173	Packard (& Packard Clipper) 264
Checker 55	Gregory 173	Playboy 273
Chevelle 56	Hoppenstand 173	Plymouth 274
Chevrolet 57	Henry J 174	Pontiac 292
Chevy II 78	Hudson 175	Pup 311
Chrysler 81	Imp 181	Rambler 311
Comet 101	Imperial 182	Riviera 324
Cord (replicar) 103	International 189	Studebaker 325
Corvair 104	Jet 192	Tasco 348
Corvette 108	Kaiser 193	Tempest 340
Crosley 110	King Midget 198	Thunderbird 344
Dart 112	Kurtis 198	Town Shopper 348
Davis 115	Lancer 199	Tucker 348
Del Mar 115	Lark 200	Valiant 349
De Soto 115	Lincoln (& Lincoln Continental) 202	Willys (& Willys Jeep) 353
Dodge 126	Marlin 213	
	Mercury 214	

WT.= 775 lbs.
(PILOT MODELS)

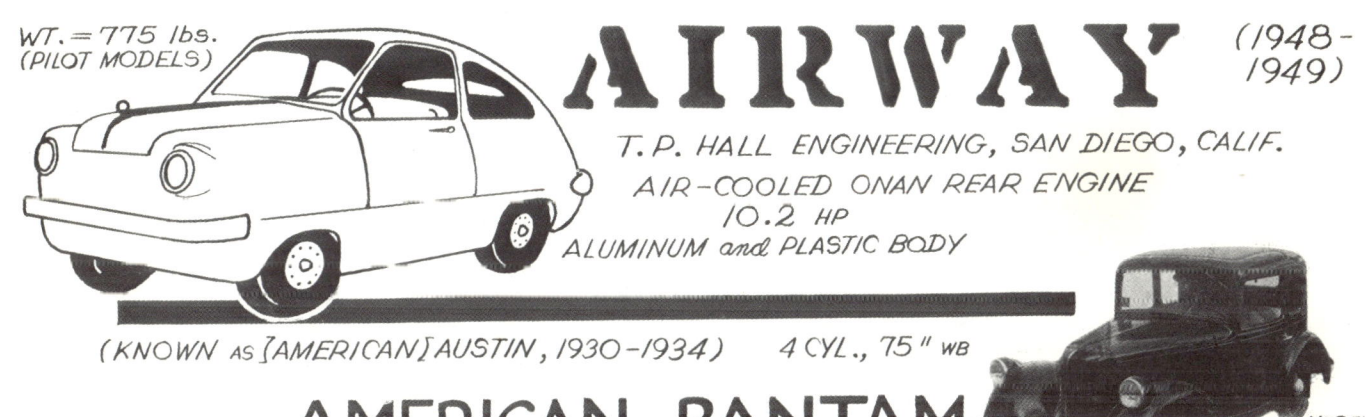

AIRWAY (1948-1949)

T. P. HALL ENGINEERING, SAN DIEGO, CALIF.
AIR-COOLED ONAN REAR ENGINE
10.2 HP
ALUMINUM and PLASTIC BODY

(KNOWN AS [AMERICAN] AUSTIN, 1930-1934)   4 CYL., 75" WB

AMERICAN BANTAM

(1935-1941) AMERICAN BANTAM CAR CO., BUTLER, PA. (OTHER BODY TYPES ALSO)

MODEL 4-65
(1940-1941)
MECH. BRAKES

ALUMINUM BODY
(1 PILOT MODEL ONLY)

BEECH PLAINSMAN
(1948)

BEECH AIRCRAFT CO., WICHITA, KAN.
4-CYL. air cooled ENGINE
also,
ELECTRIC MOTOR IN EA. WHEEL

BOBBI KAR

BOBBI MOTOR CAR CO., SAN DIEGO, CALIF.
(1945-1947)
(REPL. BY 1948 KELLER)

4-CYL. REAR ENG.

92" WB

7

Buick (ESTAB. 1903)

BUICK DIVISION OF GENERAL MOTORS
"Best buy's Buick!"

SPECIAL
SUPER
STRAIGHT-8 O.H.V. engines (SINCE '31)
LIMITED

Not a six but an EIGHT for **$895** and up

SUPER 51

WHEN BETTER AUTOMOBILES ARE BUILT, BUICK WILL BUILD THEM

MODELS:
40 SPECIAL
50 SUPER
60 CENTURY
70 ROADMASTER
80, 90 LIMITED

248 OR 320 CID
107 HP @ 3400 OR 141 HP @ 3600
(SINCE '38)

with **Body by Fisher**

Found *only* on CHEVROLET · PONTIAC · OLDSMOBILE · BUICK · CADILLAC

121, 126, 133 OR 140" WB

new SAFETY-UNIT SEALED BEAM HEADLIGHTS — brighter, longer-lasting filament in one weatherproof unit with lens and reflector — better lighting over a longer period

40

RUBY KEELER JOLSON
Here she is with her Buick Estate Wagon, smart, comfortable, useful in no end of ways, and a bargain at $1242, plus $19.50 for white sidewall tires.

SUPER 59
VARIOUS TIRE SIZES

ON DISPLAY FRIDAY
AT BUICK SHOWROOMS EVERYWHERE

BUICK

118, 121, 126 or 139" WB

Special 4-door Sedan, Model 47, $1021.

115, 125 or 165 HP

41

"Buy Buick's Best!" LIMITED

SPECIAL

('41 and EARLIER CONV'TS. HAVE NO REAR QUARTER WINDOWS)

DASH

118, 121, 124, 126, 129 or 139" WB
110, 118 or 165 HP

42-45

new "FADE-AWAY" FENDERS BLEND INTO DOORS

"Better Buy Buick"
EXEMPLAR OF GENERAL MOTORS VALUE

SPECIAL

VERTICAL BARS IN new LOWER, BROADER GRILLE

CVT., 2-DR. ROADMASTER has FULL-LENGTH FRONT FENDERS.

BUICK

PRICE RANGE: $1391. TO $2149.

DASH — CLOCK

CLOSE-UP OF SPEEDOMETER

EASILY-RESETTABLE 2ND ODOMETER RECORDS TRIP MILEAGE

ESTATE WAGON (SUPER)

SUPER

new GRILLE

46

40 SPECIAL	121" WB
50 SUPER	124"
70 ROADMASTER	129"

SUPER

REAR VIEW

ROADMASTER

10

MODEL 51 — SUPER

CONVERTIBLE *has* POWER-OPERATED TOP, SIDE WINDOWS *and* FRONT SEAT

When better automobiles are built BUICK will build them

47 $1497. TO $3030.

POSTWAR "BOMBSIGHT"-STYLE HOOD ORNAMENT (SINCE '46)

SPEC. *and* SUPER *have* 248 CID, 110 HP @ 3600 RPM

RDMSTR. *has* 320 CID, 144 HP @ 3600 RPM

MEDALLION MOVED LOWER; NOW IN TOP SECTION OF GRILLE.

Super

SUPER   SPEC.-SU.-RDMSTR. PRICES: $1735. TO $3433.

'48 SUPER *and* ROADMASTER NAMES ALSO APPEAR ON FRONT FENDERS.

48

ROADMASTER

OPTIONAL: new *Dynaflow* AUTO. TRANS.

7.00 x 15

MODEL NAME

SPECIAL (CONT'D. INTO '49)

11

BUICK

Super has 3 "PORTHOLES"

49 TOTALLY RESTYLED (EXCEPT SPECIAL)

BACK SEAT (SHOWING FOLDING ARM REST)

ROADMASTER has 4 "PORTHOLES" 150 HP

ROADMASTER with Dynaflow Drive

$1787. TO $3734.
PRICE RANGE

new DASH

"RIVIERA" (new H/T)

CVT. TOP REAR DETAIL

LATE '49 CONVERTIBLES and RIVIERAS have new "SWEEP-SPEAR" SIDE TRIM (AS ILLUSTRATED.)

12

BUICK $1856.

115 HP SPECIAL

SPECIAL INTRODUCED EARLY (IN AUG., '49)

121½" WB EXCEPT ON "52" SUPER SEDAN (125½") and ON 126½" and 130¼" RDMSTRS.

SPECIAL RETAINS 2-PC. WINDSHIELD

STARTLING new "BUMPER-GRILLE"

50

128 HP **Super**

DASH (SPC.)

THE ESTATE WAGON is yours on either SUPER or ROADMASTER chassis. Three power ranges to choose from.

BACK SEAT (SEDAN)

152 HP **ROADMASTER** RIVIERA

130¼" WB ON "RIVIERA SEDAN"

ELONGATED "PORTHOLES"

BUICK 51-52

SPECIAL ('51)

SPECIAL DE LUXE 120 TO 128 HP

ESTATE WAGON ('51)

SUPER 128 HP

DASH ('52)

ROADMASTER ('51) 152 HP

ROADMASTER ('52) 170 HP

SUPER

'52 has BROADER HUBCAP MARGINS, FULL-HEIGHT VERT. BUMPER GUARDS, NO CHROME STRIPS ALONG REAR FENDERS.

'51 BUMPER GUARDS DO NOT RUN DOWN FRONT OF BUMPER, BUT REST ON TOP.

Equipment, accessories, trim and models are subject to change without notice.

14

BUICK

FINAL STRAIGHT-8 IN SPECIAL

SPECIAL (125 HP @ 3800 RPM)

53
1903-1953

121½" WB (ALL MODELS EXC. 125½ WB RIVIERA SED.)

SPORT WIRE WH. AVAIL.

SUPER

new **V8**

322 CID ENGINE IN ALL BUT "SPECIAL"

LIMITED-PRODUCTION "SKYLARK" CVT.

164-170 HP

ROADMASTER RIVIERA

ROADMASTER (188 HP @ 4000)

BUICK

143 or 150 HP
SPECIAL

ALL V8s

195 or 200 HP
CENTURY

DASH

54

264 or 322 CID V8s
(THROUGH '55)

SKYLARK
$4483.

ROADMASTER

SUPER

ROADMASTER
200 HP @ 4100 RPM

177 or 182 HP
SUPER

16

BUICK

150 to 236 HP — ROADMASTER

TOP TO BOTTOM: SPECIAL, CENTURY, SUPER

55

DASH (SUPER)

MEDALLION GIVES 1956 DATE — SPECIAL

CENTURY

SPECIAL has 220 HP @ 4400 RPM
OTHERS, 255 HP @ 4400 RPM

SUPER

ROADMASTER

122 or 127" WB (SINCE '54)

56

322 CID V8s

new V-GRILLE (FINE HORIZ. PCS.)

BUICK

SPECIAL

CVT.

WAGON

4-DR. H/T

H/T

MODEL NAME ABOVE DIP IN SIDE CHROME TRIM (EXCEPT ON SPECIAL, WHICH HAS NO NAME HERE, OR ON SUPER (with 3 CURVED CHROME PCS. HERE.)

$3354.

CENTURY

ALL WITH *new* 364 CID ENGINE (CONT'D. IN SPECIAL and LE SABRE MODELS THROUGH 1961)

new CENTURY CABALLERO WAGON (H/T STYLE)

SUPER

CVT.

H/T

57

122" OR *new* 127½" WB (THROUGH '58)

4-DR. H/T

ROADMASTER

note UNUSUAL REAR DOOR TREATMENT ON THIS MODEL

300 HP @ 4600 RPM (EXCEPT SPECIAL, WHICH has 250 HP @ 4400) (THROUGH '58)

new CONVEX GRILLE with FINE VERTICAL PCS.

18

BUICK

new BLOCK-STYLE GRILLE

HEAVY USE of CHROME TRIM

58

SIDE "PORTHOLES" DISCONTINUED (UNTIL '60)

250-HP SPECIAL

$2820.

300 HP IN CENTURY, SUPER, RDMSTR., LIMITED

$2636.

$4557.

$5125.

SPECIAL

THE AIR BORN B-58 BUICK

SPECIAL CENTURY

CENTURY

ROADMASTER

new LIMITED (NAME REVIVED)

CVT.

BUICK

ALL-new MODEL NAMES FOR 1959: LE SABRE, INVICTA, ELECTRA, ELECTRA 225

364 CID, 250 HP @ 4400 RPM

PACE CAR AT 1959 INDY 500 RACE

LeSABRE 123" WB

LE SABRE ALL BUT (SPEC.) have 325 HP @ 4400 RPM 401 CID

INVICTA 123" WB

59 (TOTALLY RESTYLED)

DASH

new SQUARED REAR ROOFLINE ON 4-DOOR H/T.

ELECTRA 126.3" WB

CANTED HEADLIGHTS

TOP-OF-LINE ELECTRA 225 IS ILLUSTRATED.

10.5 COMPR. IN 1959

BUICK $3145. $2915.

LE SABRE
has 210, 235, 250 or 300 HP

364 CID = LE S.
401 CID = OTHERS
(SAME CHOICES IN '61)

60

A RETURN TO VARIOUS "PORTHOLE" TYPE SIDE DECORATIONS AS USED ON 1949-1956 BUICKS

new "Mirromagic" INSTRUMENT CLUSTER LETS DRIVER SEE GAUGES IN A MIRROR THAT CAN BE TILTED TO SUIT DRIVER'S OWN EYE LEVEL.

INVICTA

123" WB = LE S., INVICTA
126.3" WB = EL., EL. 225

HEADLTS. PLACED HORIZONTALLY, new GRILLE with CONCAVE VERTICAL PIECES and new 3-SHIELD BADGE

INVICTA

1960 Buick Invicta 4-Door Hardtop in Magic-Mirror Tahiti Beige and Cordovan

INVICTA and ELECTRAS have 325 HP @ 4400 RPM

ELECTRA

ELECTRA 225

$4300.

BUICK

(TOTALLY RESTYLED)
61

126" WB
ELECTRA 225
325 HP

(new ROOFLINE)

123" WB
250 HP
LE SABRE

SPECIAL-SIZE
BUICK SPECIAL
new COMPACT SERIES, STARTING 1961
SEE BUICK SPECIAL

INVICTA
123" WB   325 HP

22

BUICK

2-DR.

4447

LE SABRE

4-DR. H/T

$3567.

62

401 CID V8s (in all FULL-SIZED MODELS)

ADVANCED THRUST

I.F.S. 265 HP @ 4400
INV. 280 HP @ 4400
ELEC. 325 HP @ 4400

H/T

4-DR. H/T

INVICTA

CVT. $3815.

INVICTA ESTATE WAGON → $4034. (6-PASS.)

EL. 225 CVT.

ELECTRA 225

4-DR. H/T

H/T

ELECTRA has 126" WB (OTHERS 123")

SEDAN

Close-up of Wildcat! shows you new medallion and unique fabric overlay (available in black or white).

new 325 HP **WILDCAT!** H/T

$4125.

BUICK

SEDAN

280 HP

63 LeSABRE MODELS

$3298. 2-DR.

CVT.

WAGON with REAR-FACING 3RD SEAT

CLOSER VIEW OF LE SABRE DASH and ADDITIONAL '63 MODELS ILLUSTRATED ON NEXT PAGE.

new V-SHAPED FRONT

BUICK DASH

$4167.

INVICTA (FINAL YR.)
325 HP (ON ALL BUT LE SABRE)

note = WILDCAT has ITS OWN UNIQUE GRILLE → *Wildcat*

63 (CONT'D.)

$4047.

Electra 225

$4141.

ELECTRA TAIL-LIGHT DETAIL

25

BUICK

LE SABRE

ESTATE WAGON
210 HP

64

$3458.

$3593.

WILDCAT
325 HP

THE WILDCAT CONVERTIBLE

THE WILDCAT 4-DOOR SEDAN

WILDCAT (CLOSE-UP)

$4357.

THE ELECTRA 225 CONVERTIBLE

ELECTRA 225
325 HP

THE ELECTRA 225 4-DOOR HARDTOP

26

BUICK

LE SABRE

H/T (VINYL TOP)

123" WB
300 CID
210 HP
8.15 x 15 TIRES

LE SABRE 400

123 OR 126" WB
(SINCE '59.)

65 $3345.
TO
$4530.

4-DR. H/T

8.45 x 15 TIRES
126" WB
401 CID
325 HP

WILDCAT

H/T

SEE ALSO:
RIVIERA

CVT.

ELECTRA 225

8.85 x 15 TIRES

H/T

(INTRO. WED., OCT. 5, 1960, AS SEPARATE COMPACT SERIES OF BUICK)

SPECIAL-SIZE BUICK SPECIAL
THE BEST OF BOTH WORLDS

(and SKYLARK)

NEW!

BUICK'S REVOLUTIONARY ALUMINUM V-8. This hot 155 HP Fireball V-8 weighs just 318 pounds for a .487 horsepower to weight ratio — highest in the industry!

3 VIEWS OF SPECIAL (SEDAN)

61

WAGON has 1-PIECE SWING-UP REAR DOOR

PRICES START AT **$2659.** (STD. CPE)

SPECIAL WAGON

$3091.

112" WHEELBASE

THE CLEAN LOOK of action

BUICK **skylark**

SKYLARK is new LUXURY 185-HP MODEL of SPECIAL

SKYLARK IS AVAILABLE IN TWO-TONE OR SOLID COLORS (AS ILLUSTRATED)

$2949.

note THAT SKYLARK has OWN REAR STYLING

112" WB and 6.50 x 13 TIRES (THROUGH '63)

28

BUICK SPECIAL

SPECIAL 2-DR. CPE.

4-DR. SEDAN

SPECIAL

SPECIAL DLX.

3-SEAT WAGON $3136.

WAGON

62

185-HP V8 or new V6 ENGINE

SKYLARK

SPECIAL DE LUXE

SPECIAL 2-DR. SPORT COUPE

6.50 x 13 TIRES (SINCE '61)

WAGON

SPECIAL DE LUXE

SEDAN

$2682.

63

SKYLARK H/T

SKYLARK CVT.

29

BUICK SPECIAL DELUXE 4-DOOR SEDAN

Special 2-seat Station Wagon

SPEC.

SPEC. DLX.

210 HP

SKYLARK

new 6.50 x 14 TIRES

SKYLARK

new SPORTS WAGON

64

(9-PASS.) $3562. (CUST.)

new 115" WB

new RAISED PANORAMIC ROOF WINDOWS, AS ALSO FOUND IN new OLDS "VISTA-CRUISER" WAGON.

REAR FENDER TRIM (WAGON)

Skylark

INTERIOR VIEWS

This is the new Buick Skylark Sports Wagon. It has a raised roof so you can sit tall, and a new kind of shaded glass so you can look up and out, and a forward-facing third seat.

120" WB (WAGON)
300 CID "WILDCAT" V8

30

SPECIAL CVT.

SPECIAL SED.

BUICK SPECIAL

SKYLARK GRAN SPORT

SKYLARK GRAN SPORT

65
$2690. TO $3561.

SPECIAL 2-DR.

SKYROOF SPORTS WAG.

SKYLARK with *new* FULL-WIDTH TAIL-LIGHTS

H/T

1965 BUICK Skylark HARDTOP COUPE

(SINCE 1902) (DIV. OF **GENERAL MOTORS**)

Cadillac 40

COUPE 62

8 OR 16 CYL.

129" WB

V8 has 346 CID (SINCE '36)
135 OR 140 HP @ 3400 RPM
(SINCE '38)

DUAL DIVIDING STRIPS IN BACKLIGHT

127" WB

60 SPECIAL

V8 and V-16 PRICE RANGE OF $1685. TO $7175.
V-16 PRICED FROM $5140.

INTERIOR

THE NEW *Seventy-Two*

CADILLAC-FLEETWOOD

138" WB

FLEETWOOD 75 MODELS ALSO (141" WB)

Illustrated is the Touring Sedan for Five Passengers.

32

Cadillac Standard of the World

40 (CONT'D.)

$1240. and up final LA SALLE

185 HP @ 3600
V-16 90 SERIES
V-16 has 431 CID (SINCE '38)

LA SALLE WAS A LOWER-PRICED CADILLAC SUBSIDIARY, AVAILABLE 1927 TO 1940.

MODELS 50, 52 have 322 CID V8 (SINCE '37) 130 HP @ 3400 RPM 123" WB 7.00 x 16 TIRES

FINAL 16-CYLINDER CAR BUILT IN U.S.A.

MODEL 61 (REPLACES LA SALLE)

$4230. 60 SPECIAL

FLEETWOOD 75

new TAIL-LIGHTS

41

62 CONVERTIBLE CP. $1645.

CONVERTIBLE COUPE HAS A BACK SEAT INSIDE THE CAB. →

new FRONTAL STYLING, with BROAD, LOW GRILLE

33

Cadillac Standard of the World

60-S — SMALL VERTICAL STRIPS ON FENDERS IDENTIFY 60-S.

new HOOD RUNS TO WINDSHIELD — 62

ROUND GRILLE LIGHTS IN '42 ONLY

42-45 *Fleetwood*

MODEL "75" DOES NOT HAVE "FADE-AWAY" STYLE FENDERS (THROUGH '49.)

61

62

FLEETWOOD 60-S

46

(60-S has 5 SLOPING CHROME STRIPS ON REAR QUARTER PANEL.)

75

AS IN 1942, A TOTAL OF 6 HORIZONTAL GRILLE MEMBERS, BUT WITH new RECTANGULAR GRILLE LTS.

FRONT VIEW

Cadillac Standard of the World

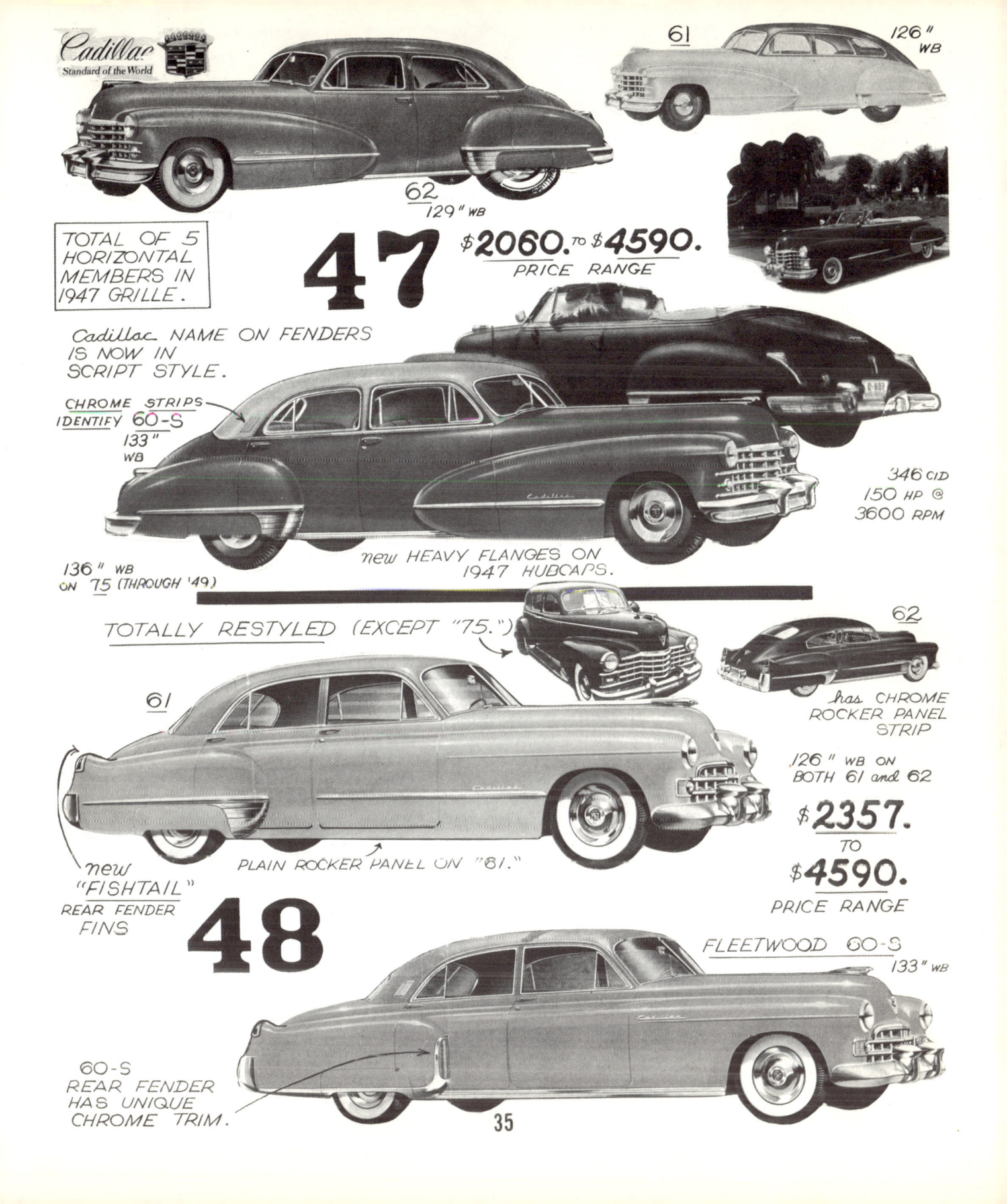

61 126" WB

62 129" WB

TOTAL OF 5 HORIZONTAL MEMBERS IN 1947 GRILLE.

47 $2060. to $4590. PRICE RANGE

Cadillac NAME ON FENDERS IS NOW IN SCRIPT STYLE.

CHROME STRIPS IDENTIFY 60-S 133" WB

346 CID 150 HP @ 3600 RPM

new HEAVY FLANGES ON 1947 HUBCAPS.

136" WB ON 75 (THROUGH '49)

TOTALLY RESTYLED (EXCEPT "75.")

62 has CHROME ROCKER PANEL STRIP

61

126" WB ON BOTH 61 and 62

$2357. TO $4590. PRICE RANGE

new "FISHTAIL" REAR FENDER FINS

PLAIN ROCKER PANEL ON "61."

48

FLEETWOOD 60-S 133" WB

60-S REAR FENDER HAS UNIQUE CHROME TRIM.

Cadillac — Standard of the World

49

61 — $2840.

IMPROVED V-8 ENGINE NOW HAS OVERHEAD VALVES.
160 HP (THROUGH '51)

...The worlds' newest engine—for the worlds' finest car!

$3103.

126" WB (61, 62)

62 — $3549.

EXCEPT ON 75, 1949 GRILLE has ONE LESS HORIZONTAL PIECE THAN 1948. new CHROME WRAP-AROUNDS EXTEND GRILLE AT EITHER END.

62

new "COUPE DE VILLE" HARDTOP CONVERTIBLE

133" WB FLEETWOOD 60 SPECIAL

$3891.

$5253.

75

"75" RETAINS OLDER STYLING. 136¼" WB

36

Cadillac Standard of the World

61

AS ILLUSTRATED, NO REAR QUARTER WINDOWS ON 61 SEDAN

122" WB

50

62

126" WB

$2761. TO $4959. PRICE RANGE

62 CVT. $3654.

new 1-PIECE WINDSHIELD

new GRILLE

60-S (130" WB)
60-S NOW has CHROME STRIPS (LOUVRES) HERE

ALL MODELS RESTYLED, INCLUDING "75."

75 (146 3/4" WB)

37

Cadillac — Standard of the World

FINAL "61" MODEL

61

62

PRICE RANGE:
$2917.
TO
$5405.

60-S

160 HP

75

51 ← new "WAFFLE" EXTENSIONS AT EITHER END OF 1951 GRILLE

38

Cadillac — Standard of the World

GOLDEN ANNIVERSARY

BEAUTIFUL NEW INTERIORS IN ALL MODELS

62 (NOW THE LOWEST-PRICED SERIES)

"V" INSIGNIA NOW COLORED GOLD, TO COMMEMORATE CADILLAC'S 50TH ANNIVERSARY.

THESE new DECORATIONS FOUND ON 1952 MODELS ONLY

1902 52
STANDARD OF THE WORLD

52

PRICE RANGE:
$3452.
TO
$5572.

147" WB
75

60-S

★ NEW 190-HORSEPOWER ENGINE
★ NEW HYDRA-MATIC DRIVE
★ NEW FRONT AND REAR END APPEARANCE
★ NEW CADILLAC POWER STEERING
★ NEW DUAL EXHAUST SYSTEM

Cadillac Standard of the World

62

126" WB

EL DORADO CVT. (new) (has WRAP-AROUND WINDSHIELD) **$7750.**

60-S $4341.
130" WB

60-S has MORE CHROME ALONG LOWER EDGE, PLUS THE CHARACTERISTIC VERTICAL STRIPS.

$4144.
62 CVT.

53
PRICE RANGE (EXC. EL D.)
$3571.
TO
$5621.

(THROUGH 1955) 331 CID ENGINE
210 HP @ 4150 RPM

LIMOUSINE
75
146.75" WB

40

Cadillac Standard of the World

62
new 129" WB

$4261.
CPE. DE VILLE

DASH (CONVERTIBLE)

new PANORAMIC WINDSHIELD

60-S
now 133" WB

54

230 HP @ 4400 RPM

75 LIMOUSINE
new 149.75" WB

EL DORADO CONVERTIBLE

41

Cadillac — Standard of the World

129" WB
62
55
250 HP @ 4600 RPM

HIGHLIGHT FEATURE of CADILLAC and OLDSMOBILE for '55!

AUTRONIC-EYE
AUTOMATIC LIGHT 'TROL

REAR VIEW

PADDED DASH DETAIL →

BRIGHT / DIM / BRIGHT
Automatically AT NIGHT!

60-S (133" WB)
(75 HAS VERTICAL CHROME STRIP RUNNING TO BOTTOM OF REAR FENDER.)

$6286.

EL DORADO
270 H.P. @ 4800 RPM
with IMPORTED, HANDCRAFTED LEATHER UPHOLSTERY

42   129" WB

Cadillac Standard of the World

CONVERT.

COUPE DE VILLE

62

60-S

PRICES START AT **$4146.**

(ACTUAL PHOTO)

LENGTH OFTEN EXAGGERATED IN ADVERTISING ART

new 365 CID (THROUGH '58) 285 HP @ 4600 RPM

56

FINER MEMBERS IN GRILLE

LIMOUSINE

75 **$6773.**

SEVILLE

Eldorado

BIARRITZ CVT.

$6501. FOR EITHER MODEL OF EL DORADO

305 H.P.

43

Cadillac Standard of the World $4677. TO $13,074. PRICE RANGE (new EL.D. BRGH. IS COSTLIEST MODEL.)

60-S

new SQUARED-OFF TAIL-FINS with LOW, ROUND TAIL-LIGHTS

REAR BRIGHTWORK PANELS ON 60-S

'57

EL DORADO BIARRITZ (325 HP)

62 300 HP

EL DORADO (BROUGHAM - 4 DR.) (SEVILLE - 2 DR.)

new GRILLE

ALL '58 MODELS have BACK-SLANTING FINS, AS SEEN ON '57 EL DORADO.

129½ WB
310 HP

58

FOUR HEADLIGHTS

new LOWER, BROADER GRILLE

MORE 1958 MODELS ON NEXT PAGE

44

Cadillac
STANDARD OF THE WORLD

60-S CONTINUES LOWER BRIGHTWORK PANELS ON REAR FENDERS. 133" WB

AS IN 1957, EL DORADO BROUGHAM HAS ITS OWN UNIQUE FRONT END STYLING. **$13,074.**

$7500. FOR SEVILLE OR BIARR.

58 (CONT'D.)

note ROUNDED-DOWN REAR FENDER/DECK PANELS only on THESE 2 ELDORADO TYPES.

EL DORADO SEVILLE
(335 HP, 129½" WB ON EL DORADOS)

EL DORADO BIARRITZ

(149¾" WB ON 75)

45

Cadillac STANDARD OF THE WORLD

ENORMOUS TAIL-FINS!

new "DOUBLE-DECK" GRILLE

DETAILS OF THE UNIQUE REAR END DESIGN IN 1959

CLOSER VIEW OF TRADITIONAL "V" ON REAR DECK

GRILLE MOTIF IS ALSO CARRIED ON AT REAR

59

325 HP (THROUGH '63)   130" WB

NOTE THE ROOFLINE DIFFERENCES BETWEEN THESE 4-DOOR HARDTOPS

1959 PRICES START AT $4892.

2 DR. H/T
DE VILLE

'59 HP FIGS. @ 4800 RPM
new 390 CID V8s

FLEETWOOD 75 (149.87" WB)

LIMOUSINE $9748.

(CONT'D.)

59
(CONT'D.)

Cadillac — Standard of the World

FLEETWOOD
60 SPECIAL
(note ITS
OWN UNIQUE
SIDE and FENDER
TRIM)

$6233.

note "FLEETWOOD" NAME
ON FRONT FENDER PANEL. (60-S)

DASH

345-HP
EL DORADO MODELS BELOW:

("ELDORADO" NAME
on FRONT FENDER
PANELS of
BIARRITZ and
SEVILLE ONLY.)
$7401. (EITHER MODEL)

BIARRITZ

BROUGHAM

EL DORADO
BROUGHAM STYLING
DIFFERS FROM
OTHER 1959
CADILLACS.
$13,075.

SEVILLE

47

Cadillac — STANDARD OF THE WORLD

62 — new 1-PC. GRILLE

PICTURED AT BOCA RATON HOTEL and CLUB, FLORIDA

60

PRICES START AT $**4892**. FOR 2-DR. 62 H/T (ILLUSTR.)

$**6233**. 60-S

62

SEDAN DE VILLE

62

TAIL-FINS REDUCED FOR '60, IN STYLE OF '59 EL DORADO BROUGHAM.

(CONT'D.)

48

FLEETWOOD 75
9-PASS. SEDAN
$9533.

$9748.
60 PRICE OF 75 LIMO. (ILLUSTR. AT LEFT)
(CONT'D.)

FLEETWOOD 75 LIMOUSINE

EL DORADO BROUGHAM
(SAME PRICES AS IN 1959 ON ALL 3 EL DORADOS)

EL DORADO SEVILLE

FINAL H/T EL DORADOS UNTIL 1967, AT WHICH TIME EL DORADO BECOMES A SPECIAL FRONT-WHEEL-DRIVE 2-DR. H/T.

note THAT THE EL DORADO BROUGHAM has SIDE TRIM DIFFERENT FROM THAT OF THE OTHER EL DORADO MODELS OF 1960.

EL DORADO BIARRITZ
(EL DO. CVT. CONT'D. THROUGH '66)

49

375 HP

62

new LOWER SIDE FIN, TO BALANCE EFFECT OF UPPER TAIL FIN

61 new 129½" WB RESTYLED, SLIGHTLY DOWNSIZED and LIGHTENED

new CONVEX GRILLE

62

$4892. TO $9748. PRICE RANGE

CHROME BANDS NEAR END OF REAR FENDER IDENTIFY 60-S.

FLEETWOOD 60-S
$6233.

50

Cadillac — STANDARD OF THE WORLD

DASH

RADIO, CLOCK DETAIL

62

SEDAN DE VILLE

COUPE

$5752.

$5189.

Fog Lamps (OPT.)

$10,100.

FLEETWD. 60-S BACK SEAT

FLEETWOOD 75 LIMO.

REAR COMPARTMENT (75)

$6529.

note CONVERTIBLE-TOP STYLING ON HARDTOP.

62

PRICE RANGE: $5191. TO $10,104.

FLEETWOOD 75
9-PASS.

FLEETWOOD 60-S

62

"FLEETWOOD" ON 60-S FENDER

DASH

REAR CLOSE-UP

EL DORADO BIARRITZ

63

HEAD-ON DETAIL OF LIGHTS IN RELATION TO GRILLE

new 340 HP (62 SERIES ONLY)

new GRILLE EMPHASIZES "DOUBLE-DECK" STYLING.

52

Cadillac
STANDARD OF THE WORLD

DASH AND INTERIOR VIEWS

new "COMFORT CONTROL"

new CONVEX GRILLE

64

ALL MODELS NOW HAVE 340 HP @ 4600 RPM and now 429 CID

75

"62" PRICES FROM $5191.

Comfort Control combines heating and air conditioning in a single unit, the interior weather never changes. Even humidity is under perfect control. This system now available as an extra-cost option.

53

Cadillac

CALAIS (REPLACES 62 SER.)

DE VILLE

FLEETWOOD BROUGHAM

65 new TAIL-LIGHTS

PRICE RANGE: $5224. TO $10,125.

new LARGE 1-PC. GRILLE

new VERTICALLY-PLACED HEADLIGHTS

DASH

RADIO DETAIL

CHECKER

CHECKER MOTORS CORPORATION
Kalamazoo, Michigan

SINCE 1922

1947 TO 1955 STYLE →

1956 TO 1958 STYLE →

TAXIS, COMMERCIAL ONLY (THROUGH '58)

Checker Aerobus Limousine

CHRYSLER V8 ENGINE IN PRE-'64 AEROBUS

6-CYL. CONTINENTAL ENGINE USED (UNTIL '63.) STARTING 1964, CHEVROLET 6 OR V8.

DASH ('68)

Checker Marathon Deluxe Limousine

59 ON

NO YEARLY STYLE CHANGES. OCCASIONAL MINOR MODIFICATIONS.

120" WB

Checker Marathon 4-door sedan

INTERIOR ('69)

SAFETY-BUMPERS (ENERGY-ABSORBING) ADDED IN MID-1970s.

Checker Marathon 4-door station wagon

55

CHEVELLE (NEW) by Chevrolet

(2-DR. WAGON ALSO AVAIL.)

INTERIOR (MALIBU)

64
194 or 230 CID 6 (120 or 155 HP @ 4400 RPM)
ALSO 283 CID V8 (195 or 220 HP @ 4800 RPM)

MALIBU
115" W.B.

300
300 DELUXE
300 2-DR.
300 2-DR. 6-PASS. WAGON (MALIBU 4-DR. WAGON has CHROME STRIP ALONG SIDE.)

MALIBU SS

new HORIZONTALLY-SPLIT GRILLE

65
194 or 230 CID 6 (120 or 140 HP @ 4400 RPM)
ALSO:
(283 CID V8 AVAIL. ONLY WITH 195 HP @ 4800 RPM)
3 new 327 CID V8s (250, 300, or 350 HP)

56

BODY by FISHER
GM
CHEVROLET
(EST. 1911)
SINCE 1912
6 CYL.
(SINCE '29)
SPEC. DLX.
DASH
MINE FOR
1940
note
LIGHTS PARTIALLY
SUNK INTO FENDERS
MASTER 85 HAS STRAIGHT
FRONT AXLE,
OTHERS have
"KNEE
ACTION."
MASTER
DE LUXE
COUPE
COACH
new
113" WB
The Special De Luxe Sport Sedan, $802*
new "BANNER" TYPE
WIDE GRILLE
SEDAN
(MASTER 85
ENDS '40)
MASTER DLX.
and SPEC.
DLX. ARE
CONT'D.
THROUGH
'41
USA-1
1940
Let This Power Cylinder
Shift for You!
$659
MASTER 85
BUSINESS COUPE
Only Chevrolet has the New Exclusive Vacuum-Power Shift . . . the only steering column gearshift that does 80% of the work for you and requires only 20% driver effort!
KB, KH, KA
40
(RESTYLED)
6.00 × 16 TIRES
(SINCE '37)
216.5 CID
85 HP @
3200 RPM
(SINCE '37)
CVT.
CHEVROLET
EYE IT . . . TRY IT . . . BUY IT!

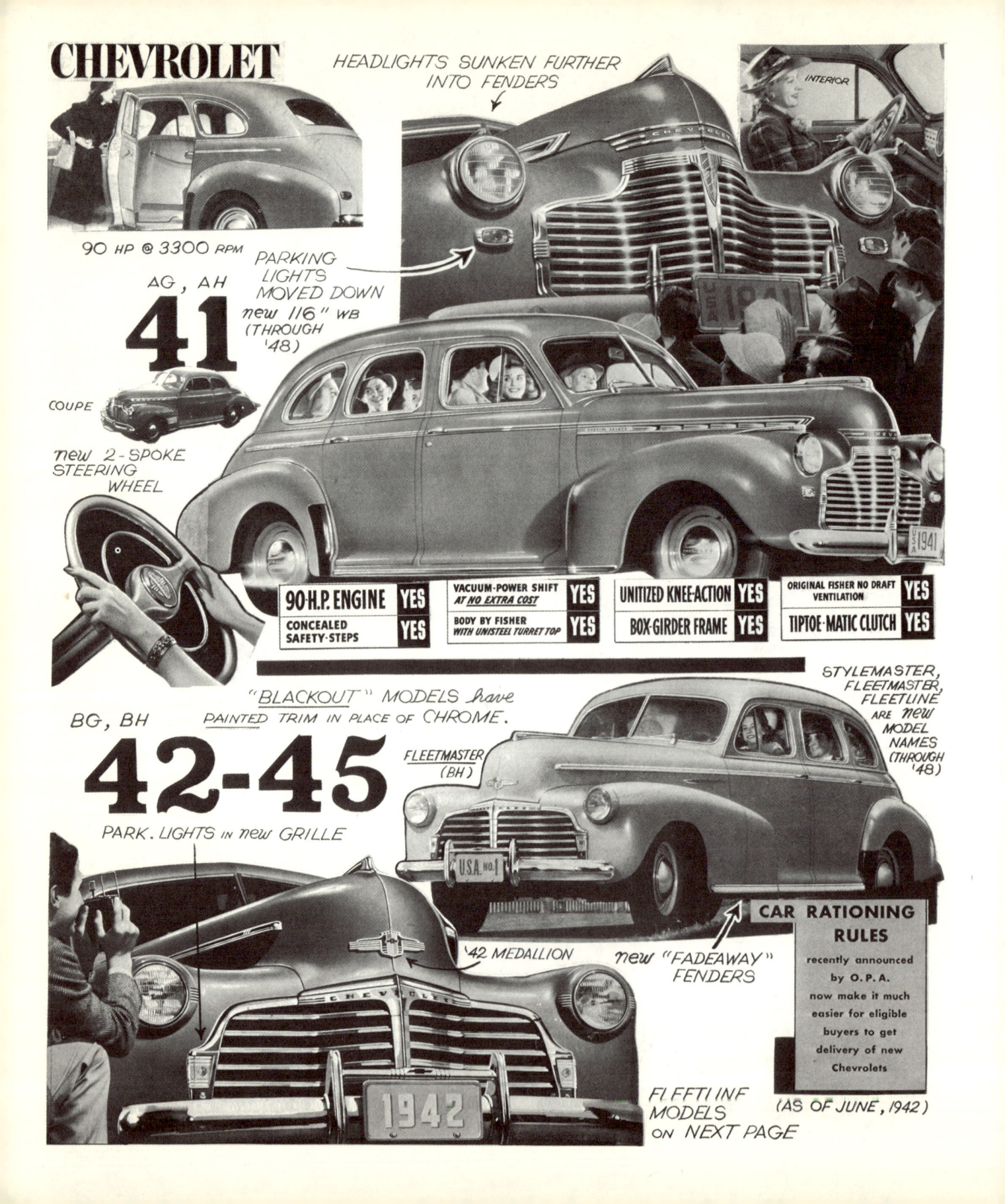

CHEVROLET

HEADLIGHTS SUNKEN FURTHER INTO FENDERS

INTERIOR

90 HP @ 3300 RPM

AG, AH

41

PARKING LIGHTS MOVED DOWN

new 116" WB (THROUGH '48)

COUPE

new 2-SPOKE STEERING WHEEL

| 90·H.P. ENGINE | YES | VACUUM-POWER SHIFT AT NO EXTRA COST | YES | UNITIZED KNEE·ACTION | YES | ORIGINAL FISHER NO DRAFT VENTILATION | YES |
| CONCEALED SAFETY·STEPS | YES | BODY BY FISHER WITH UNISTEEL TURRET TOP | YES | BOX·GIRDER FRAME | YES | TIPTOE·MATIC CLUTCH | YES |

BG, BH

42-45

"BLACKOUT" MODELS have PAINTED TRIM IN PLACE OF CHROME.

FLEETMASTER (BH)

STYLEMASTER, FLEETMASTER, FLEETLINE ARE new MODEL NAMES (THROUGH '48)

PARK. LIGHTS IN new GRILLE

'42 MEDALLION

new "FADEAWAY" FENDERS

CAR RATIONING RULES recently announced by O.P.A. now make it much easier for eligible buyers to get delivery of new Chevrolets

(AS OF JUNE, 1942)

FLEETLINE MODELS ON NEXT PAGE

CHEVROLET

$880.

NEW CHEVROLET *Fleetline* AEROSEDAN

2 New "FLEETLINE" (BH) MODELS EASILY IDENTIFIED BY 3 HORIZONTAL CHROME STRIPS ON EACH FENDER (THROUGH '48)

NEW CHEVROLET *Fleetline* SPORTMASTER

42-45 (CONT'D.)

SLOGAN: "THE FINEST CHEVROLET OF ALL TIME"

$920.

DK "FLEETMASTER" has CHROME TRIM AROUND WINDOW MOULDINGS

PRICE RANGE: **$1022.** TO **$1614.**

DJ, DK **46** new GRILLE

DJ "STYLEMASTER" (NO CHROME ON WINDOW OR WINDSHIELD MOULDINGS.)

$1194. SPORT SEDAN

'46 MEDALLION

59

CHEVROLET

$1255.

216.5 CID
90 HP @ 3300 RPM
116" WB

EK FLEETMASTER

new GRILLE has PROTRUDING CENTER SECTION

EJ, EK **47**

$1775.

new MEDALLION

FLEETMASTER CVT.

EK FLEETLINE AERO

EK FLEETLINE SPORTMASTER

$1525.

FJ STYLEMASTER

FK 1948 CHEVROLET "FLEETMASTER" Four Door Sedan

$1340.

FK FLEETLINE AERO

FJ, FK **48**

new "T"-SHAPED PIECE ADDED AT CENTER OF GRILLE

PRICE RANGE: $1160. TO $1890.

PACE CAR AT 1948 INDY 500 RACE

CHEVROLET

METAL-BODIED WAGON

2-DR. FLEETLINE 4-DR.

PRICES START AT $1339.

GJ, GK
49
TOTALLY RESTYLED

GJ = SPECIAL
GK = DE LUXE

1949 TRUNK LID has SMALL "T" HANDLE which TURNS.

2-DR. TOWN SEDAN

4-DR. SPORT SEDAN

STYLELINE SPORT CPE.

VERTICAL PIECES in LOWER HALF of GRILLE

new SHORTER 115" WB (THROUGH '57)

1949 HUBCAP has RED CENTER.
6.70 x 15

all-new INTERIOR (LEFT and RIGHT VIEWS)

PONTOON-STYLE REAR FENDERS

DLX. MODELS have CHROME AROUND WINDOWS and on FRONT FENDERS

CHROME (DLX.)
BLACK RUBBER (SPEC.)

61

CHEVROLET $1741.

new "Bel-Air" 2-DR. HARDTOP has WIDE BACKLIGHT

DASH

1950 TRUNK LID has new RE-DESIGNED HANDLE.

STYLING SIMILAR TO 1949, EXCEPT FOR MINOR DIFFERENCES AS NOTED.

new AUTOMATIC TRANSMISSION AVAILABLE

HJ, HK

50

new 1950 GRILLE WITHOUT VERTICAL LOWER CENTER PCS. SEEN IN '49.

HJ = SPECIAL
HK = DE LUXE

First low-priced car with POWER*Glide* No-Shift driving *

PRICE RANGE: $1329. TO $1994.

* = POWERGLIDE SOMEWHAT LIKE BUICK'S "DYNAFLOW." (NOT INCLUDED IN ABOVE PRICES)

BACK SEAT (4-DR.)

The Styleline De Luxe 2-Door Sedan

1950 HUBCAP has YELLOW CENTER.

62

CHEVROLET

BEL-AIR $1914.

FLEETLINE

STYLELINE DE LUXE

STYLELINE PRICES START AT $1460.

JJ, JK
51

GRILLE CHANGED

INTERIOR VIEWS

NEW Safety-Sight Instrument Panel

NEW Modern-Mode Interiors

STYLELINE DE LUXE

new CHROME TRIM STYLE

CHEVROLET

$1696.

STYLELINE SPECIAL
(has MINIMUM OF CHROME TRIM)

FLEETLINE DLX.
(NO MORE FLEETLN. SPECIAL)

NEW

52
KJ, KK

STYLELINE DE LUXE 2-DR.

26 Exterior Colors and two-tone color combinations to choose from.

New Softer, Smoother Ride with new and improved shock absorber action.

Improved Carburetion with Automatic Choke in Powerglide models.

New Centerpoise Power is smoother — "screens out" engine vibration.

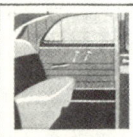

Color-Matched Two-Tone Interiors bring new beauty to De Luxe models.

new 5 RIDGES RUN DOWN CENTER HORIZ. MEMBER OF GRILLE.

new MEDALLION

$1519. TO $2281.
PRICE RANGE

STYLELINE DE LUXE SPORT COUPE (ABOVE)

(2 VIEWS)

$1992.

BEL AIR (IN STYLELINE DLX. SERIES) H/T

FINAL YEAR FOR STYLELINE and FLEETLINE MODEL NAMES.

CHEVROLET

150

AT RIGHT: 210 SEDAN
(IN SAN FRANCISCO, CALIF.) →

210 2-DR.

BEL AIR SEDAN (INTERIOR)

53 (TOTALLY RESTYLED)

"Handyman" (two of them) 6-PASS. **150** station wagons

210

BEL AIR (note EXTRA TRIM and CONTRASTING COLOR STRIP on REAR FENDER.)

BEL AIR now TOP-OF-LINE SERIES WHICH INCLUDES 2-DR. SEDAN, 4-DR. SEDAN, CONVERTIBLE (ILLUSTRATED) and H/T SPORT COUPE (ILLUSTRATED)

235 CID ENGINE (THROUGH '62, ON 6-CYL.) 108 OR 115 HP @ 3600 RPM)

WITH IMITATION WOODGRAIN TRIM

Townsman 8-PASS.

65

CHEVROLET

new MEDALLION
new TAIL-LIGHTS

54

Advanced Chevrolet Engineering brings
CYBERNETIC CHEVROLET
(Cybernetic = Automatic Control)

210 DELRAY COUPE

BEL AIR

115 HP @ 3700 RPM
OR 125 HP @ 4000 RPM

new OBLONG PARK. LIGHTS

new GRILLE has 5 VERTICAL PCS.
INSTEAD OF 3

CHEVROLET

150
$1593.

"ONE-FIFTY" HANDYMAN

2 VIEWS OF DASH

210 HANDYMAN

BEL AIR

THE "TWO-TEN" 4-DOOR SEDAN in Skyline Blue.

(TOTALLY RESTYLED) **55**

new V-8 ALSO AVAIL. (265 CID, 162 HP @ 4400 RPM OR 180 HP @ 4600 RPM) 6 CYL. has 123 HP @ 3800 OR 136 HP @ 4200 RPM)

210 "TOWNSMAN" WAGON

THE BEL AIR BEAUVILLE

new "NOMAD" 2 DR. WAGON

(CHROME STRIPS RUNNING DOWN TAILGATE.)

CVT. IS PACE CAR AT 1955 INDY 500 RACE

$2472. (6)

CHEVROLET

THE "ONE-FIFTY" HANDYMAN
2 doors, 6 passengers, versatile and thrifty.

56

THE "TWO-TEN" HANDYMAN
2 doors, 6 passengers, all-vinyl interior.

THE "TWO-TEN" BEAUVILLE
4 doors, 9 passengers.

THE "TWO-TEN" TOWNSMAN
4 doors, 6 passengers, loads of cargo space.

BEL AIR 4-DOOR HARDTOP and interior

AIR COND. DETAIL

Now in the low price field... $2329.

All components are located "up front"... out of sight and out of the way! Harrison air conditioning is available on four great GM cars—Chevrolet, Pontiac, Oldsmobile and Buick.

AIR CONDITIONING!

BEL AIR BEAUVILLE 9-PASS. WAGON

new SMALL ROUND LENSES IN TAIL-LIGHTS

210

6.70 x 15 TIRES

BEL AIR SEDAN
140, 162, 170, 205 OR 225 HP

CORVETTE

NOMAD

new FULL-WIDTH GRILLE

BEL AIR 2-DR.

68

CHEVROLET

PRICES START AT $1885.

new 7.50 x 14 TIRES

150

210

BEL AIR

1957 IS 3RD AND FINAL YEAR THAT THE NOMAD IS A SUPER-DELUXE 2-DOOR SPORT WAGON.

$2757. (6)

NEW TRIPLE-TURBINE TURBOGLIDE*
It's the last word in automatic drives. Super-smooth— and there's even a HILL RETARDER position on the selector, for safer control on the steepest down grades!

57

NOMAD and BEL AIR have new ANODIZED REAR FENDER PANEL.

4-DOOR WAGON

new GRILLE COMBINED with BUMPER

2-DR. H/T

BEL AIR

COMMAND POST CONTROL PANEL

HEADLIGHT-HOOD AIR VENTS

$2464.

4-DR. H/T

140, 162, 185, 220, 245, 250, 270 or 283 HP
(new 283 CID V8 JOINS 265 CID)

CHEVROLET

NOMAD 6-PASS. 4-DR.

DASH

BEL AIR

4-DR., 6 OR 9-PASS. BROOKWOOD

new 117½" WB (1958 ONLY)

BISCAYNE

235 CID 6 has 145 HP @ 4200 RPM

58

2-DR. 6-PASS. YEOMAN

CROSS-SECTION OF "TURBO THRUST" V8 ENGINE
283 OR 348 CID V8s (TO '62) (185 TO 280 HP)

new IMPALA $2693.

new WAGON TAILGATE

IMPALAS have 6 REAR LIGHTS, AND EXTRA "AIR SCOOP" DECORATIONS.

CHEVROLET

1 — *Biscayne Utility Sedan.* Chevy's prices start right here — a handy, handsome 2-door with 31 cu. ft. of cargo space behind front seat.

2 — *Brookwood 2-Door*, Chevrolet's lowest priced wagon, is as dutiful as it is beautiful. Seats 6, holds up to 92 cu. ft. of cargo.

3 — *Impala 4-Door*, most elegant family sedan in the line, makes you wonder why anyone would want a car that costs more.

4 — *El Camino* combines stunning passenger car styling with the load space of a pickup. Good looks never carried so much weight!

5 — *Impala Convertible.* Chevy's got a special formula for carefree top-down fun.

6 — *Biscayne 2-Door.* This beauty's the lowest priced 6-passenger Chevy you can buy!

7 — *Nomad 4-Door*, 6-passenger station wagon — finest of Chevrolet's 5 wonderful wagons.

8 — *Bel Air 4-Door.* As luxurious as it looks, yet priced just above Chevy's thriftiest sedans.

9 — *Brookwood 4-Door.* Chevy's lowest priced 4-door wagon seats 6, holds 92 cu. ft. of cargo with rear seat down.

10 — *Bel Air 2-Door*, distinctively styled inside and out, carries a price tag just a notch above Chevy's thriftiest 2-door sedan.

11 — *Impala Sport Sedan.* Here's a 4-door hardtop with the kind of looks and luxury you'd expect only on the most expensive makes.

12 — *Kingswood 4-Door*, 9-passenger station wagon, offers rear-facing third seat and power-operated rear window at no extra cost.

13 — *Impala Sport Coupe.* It's one of Chevy's full series of elegant Impalas for '59. And you won't find a handsomer hardtop anywhere!

14 — *Parkwood 4-Door*, 6-passenger station wagon, distinctively trimmed inside and out, priced a shade above the thrifty Brookwoods.

15 — *Bel Air Sport Sedan.* It's Chevy's lowest priced hardtop — and it makes beautiful sense!

16 — *Corvette.* Take the wheel of America's only authentic sports car and treat yourself to the snappiest, happiest driving you've known.

17 — *Biscayne 4-Door*, thriftiest 4-door sedan in the line, is another big reason.

BROOKWOOD

135 TO 315 HP

PRICE RANGE $2160. TO $3009.

BEL AIR

NOMAD 4 DR., 6-PASS.

HUGE new TAIL-LIGHTS

59
(TOTALLY RESTYLED)

new 119" WB (THROUGH '70)

BIG "GULL WING" REAR DECK

71 IMPALA SPORT COUPE (H/T)

CHEVROLET

BISCAYNE

NOMAD

KINGSWOOD

60

PRICE RANGE: $2230. TO $2996.

BEL AIR

BEL AIR

new GRILLE

IMPALA SPORT CPE.

Impala 4-Door Sport Sedan

135 TO 335 HP

MODIFIED "GULL-WING" REAR STYLING, *with* new ROUND TAIL-LIGHTS

72

CHEVROLET

BROOKWOOD

BISCAYNE

135 TO 360 HP

NOMAD

new ROOFLINE (SPT. CPE.)

BEL AIR

IMPALA (RESTYLED)
61
$2230.
TO $3099.
PRICE RANGE

(HT) SPT. CPE.

new ROOFLINE → BEL AIR SPT. SED.

DASH

LIGHT CONTROL SWITCH — CIGARETTE LIGHTER AND ASH TRAY — RADIO CONTROLS

LEFT VENT CONTROL — WIPER AND WASHER CONTROL — HEATER CONTROLS — RIGHT VENT CONTROL — IGNITION SWITCH — GLOVE BOX AND LOCK

IMPALA

73

BISCAYNE

CHEVROLET

FINAL 235 CID
6 has
135 HP @
4000
RPM

BEL AIR SPT. CPE. ROOFLINE

DASH

BEL AIR

new GRILLE

IMPALA
283, new 327 or
new 409 CID
V8s
(170
to
409
HP)

IMPALA has ALUMINIZED PANELING AROUND TAIL-LIGHTS

OUTER-EDGE TAIL-LTS. DO NOT OPEN with TRUNK.

IMPALA

62

(IMPALA I.D.)

JET-SMOOTH RIDE

74

BISCAYNE

DASH

IMPALA SPORT SEDAN

BEL AIR

PRICE RANGE: $2558. TO $3417.

63

new 230 CID 6 (140 HP @ 4400 RPM.

IMPALA

note CONVERTIBLE-STYLE "CREASES" STAMPED INTO STEEL ROOF of this IMPALA SPORT COUPE.

V8s have 19.5 HP @ 4800 to 425 HP @ 6000

new DIP IN MIDDLE OF DECK LID ON 1963 MODELS.

1964 JET-SMOOTH CHEVROLET

BISCAYNE

BISCAYNE

BISCAYNE

BEL AIR

new STRAIGHT-ACROSS DECK LID with CENTER RIDGE

2-DR. BISCAYNE $2590.

64

283, 327, 409 or V8 ENGINES, SAME SIZES AS IN '63
6 = 140 HP
V8s = 195, 250, 300, 340, 400 or 425 HP

3.08 to 4.56 GEAR RATIOS

SPT. SEDAN 4-DR. H/T

9-PASS. WAGON

IMPALA

IMPALA SS
H/T

new IMPALA SS $3185.

ONE OF VARIOUS 1964 UPHOLSTERY PATTERNS

new GRILLE

DASH

CHEVROLET $2669.. 4 DOOR BISCAYNE

7.35 x 14 TIRES

BEL AIR

IMPALA

IMPALA 3-SEAT WAGON

$3444..

8.25 x 14 TIRES ON WAGONS

IMPALA DASH

LIGHTS — VENT — WIPER WASHER — IGNITION SWITCH — LIGHTER — ASH TRAY — RADIO — HEATER — GLOVE BOX — VENT

POPULARLY REFERRED TO AS THE "COKE BOTTLE" PROFILE

H/T

IMPALA SUPER SPORT

65 (TOTALLY RESTYLED)

AVAIL. with VINYL TOP

with SPORT WHEEL COVERS →

$3210..

Chevy II

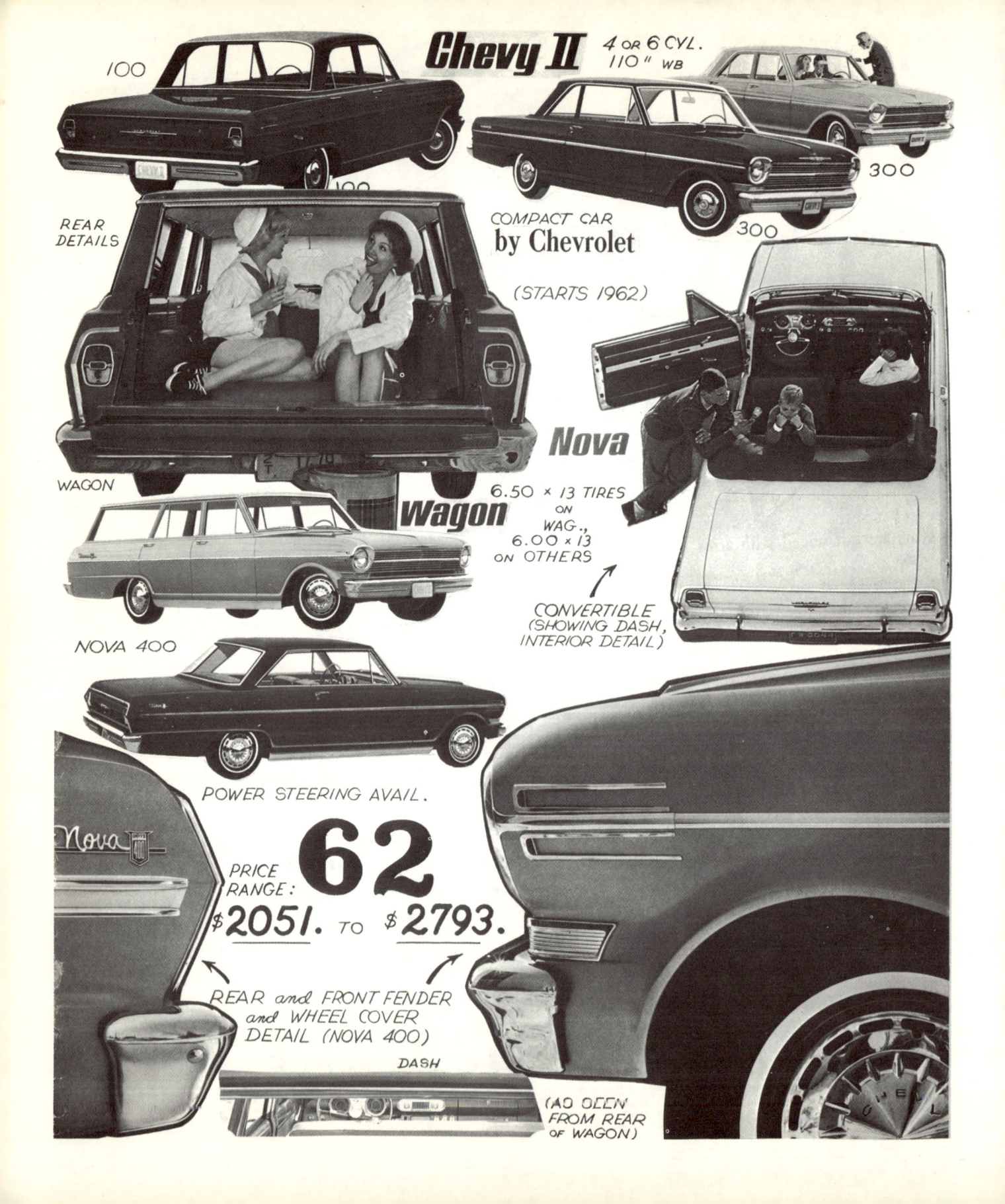

100

4 or 6 CYL.
110" WB

300

300

REAR DETAILS

COMPACT CAR by Chevrolet

(STARTS 1962)

Nova

WAGON

Wagon

6.50 × 13 TIRES ON WAG., 6.00 × 13 ON OTHERS

NOVA 400

CONVERTIBLE (SHOWING DASH, INTERIOR DETAIL)

POWER STEERING AVAIL.

PRICE RANGE: **62**
$2051. TO $2793.

REAR and FRONT FENDER and WHEEL COVER DETAIL (NOVA 400)

DASH

(AS SEEN FROM REAR OF WAGON)

CHEVY II

100

$2313.

300

$2395.

$2710.

63

NOVA 400

new GRILLE

120 HP
(6 CYL.)
(SINCE '62)

NEW V8 POWER (OPTIONAL)

64   4, 6, or V8

MORE '64s ON NEXT PAGE

79

CHEVY II

INTERIOR

64 (CONT'D.)

SPT. CPE.

NOVA SS (has THIS EMBLEM)

NOVA

SEDAN

Super Sport

(TAILGATE OPEN)

NOVA

(TAILGATE CLOSED)

65

SEE ALSO: Chevrolet

80

CHRYSLER

CHRYSLER CORPORATION

(EST. 1924)

DASH

FLUID DRIVE'S MAGIC

new GRILLE (9 HORIZ. PIECES)

ROYAL and WINDSOR 6 have 241.5 CID (THROUGH '41) 108 HP @ 3600 RPM

122½" WB (ROYAL + WND.)

ROYAL 6 (C-25 S)
C-25 (6-CYL.)

'40

$895*
3-PASS. ROYAL COUPE

C-26 (8-CYL.)

AMERICA'S FIRST FLUID DRIVE!
The vanes of the driving member force the fluid against those of the driven member, thus transmitting the power without a rigid metal connection. Incredibly smooth.

ONLY $38 EXTRA

ALSO AVAILABLE ON THE NEW YORKER AND SARATOGA MODELS
STANDARD ON CROWN IMPERIAL

Traveler 8 (C-26 K) (MADE IN 1940 ONLY)

HIGHLANDER (6 or 8) has SCOTTISH PLAID UPHOLSTERY

TRAVELER, SARATOGA and NEW YORKER 8   128½" WB
323.5 CID (THROUGH '50)
135 HP @ 3400 RPM (THR. '49)

Be Modern – Buy Chrysler!

CHRYSLER

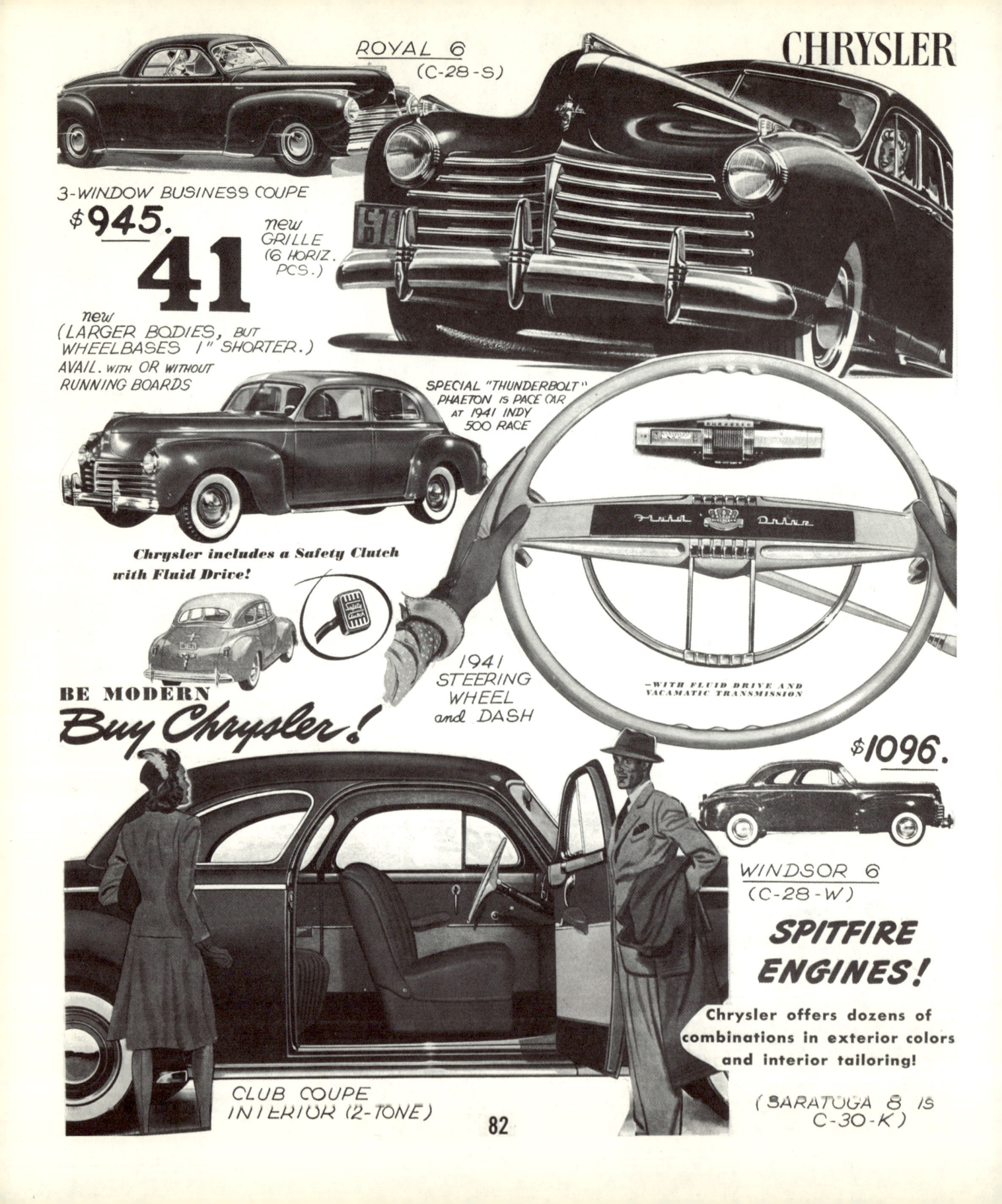

ROYAL 6
(C-28-S)

3-WINDOW BUSINESS COUPE
$945.

41

new GRILLE (6 HORIZ. PCS.)

new (LARGER BODIES, BUT WHEELBASES 1" SHORTER.)
AVAIL. WITH OR WITHOUT RUNNING BOARDS

SPECIAL "THUNDERBOLT" PHAETON IS PACE CAR AT 1941 INDY 500 RACE

Chrysler includes a Safety Clutch with Fluid Drive!

1941 STEERING WHEEL and DASH

—WITH FLUID DRIVE AND VACAMATIC TRANSMISSION

BE MODERN
Buy Chrysler!

$1096.

WINDSOR 6
(C-28-W)

SPITFIRE ENGINES!

Chrysler offers dozens of combinations in exterior colors and interior tailoring!

CLUB COUPE INTERIOR (2-TONE)

(SARATOGA 8 IS C-30-K)

CHRYSLER 41 (CONT'D.)

TOWN and COUNTRY (new)

$2795.

NEW YORKER HIGHLANDER 8 CONVT. (C-30-N)

PLAID UPHOLSTERY OPTIONAL @ EXTRA COST

WHEEL COVER

CROWN IMPERIAL 8 LIMOUSINE (C-33)

$1495.

ENGINE

TOWN and COUNTRY

DASH

42-45
C-34 (6)
C-36 (8)

(CROWN IMPERIAL is C-37.)

new "BEAUTY RINGS"

new "WRAP-AROUND" GRILLE

Fluid Drive and Vacamatic Transmission!

83

CHRYSLER

ROYAL 6 (C-38-S)
WINDSOR 6,
TOWN and COUNTRY 6
 (C-38-W)
SARATOGA 8 (C-39-K)
NEW YORKER 8,
TOWN and COUNTRY 8
 (C-39-N)
CROWN IMPERIAL 8
 (C-40)

EMBLEM
Chrysler

CHRYSLER CARS CONTINUE USE OF ADD-ON WHITE "BEAUTY RINGS," THUS MAKING UNNECESSARY THE USE OF HARD-TO-OBTAIN WHITE SIDEWALL TIRES.

PRICE RANGE:
$1415. TO $4767.

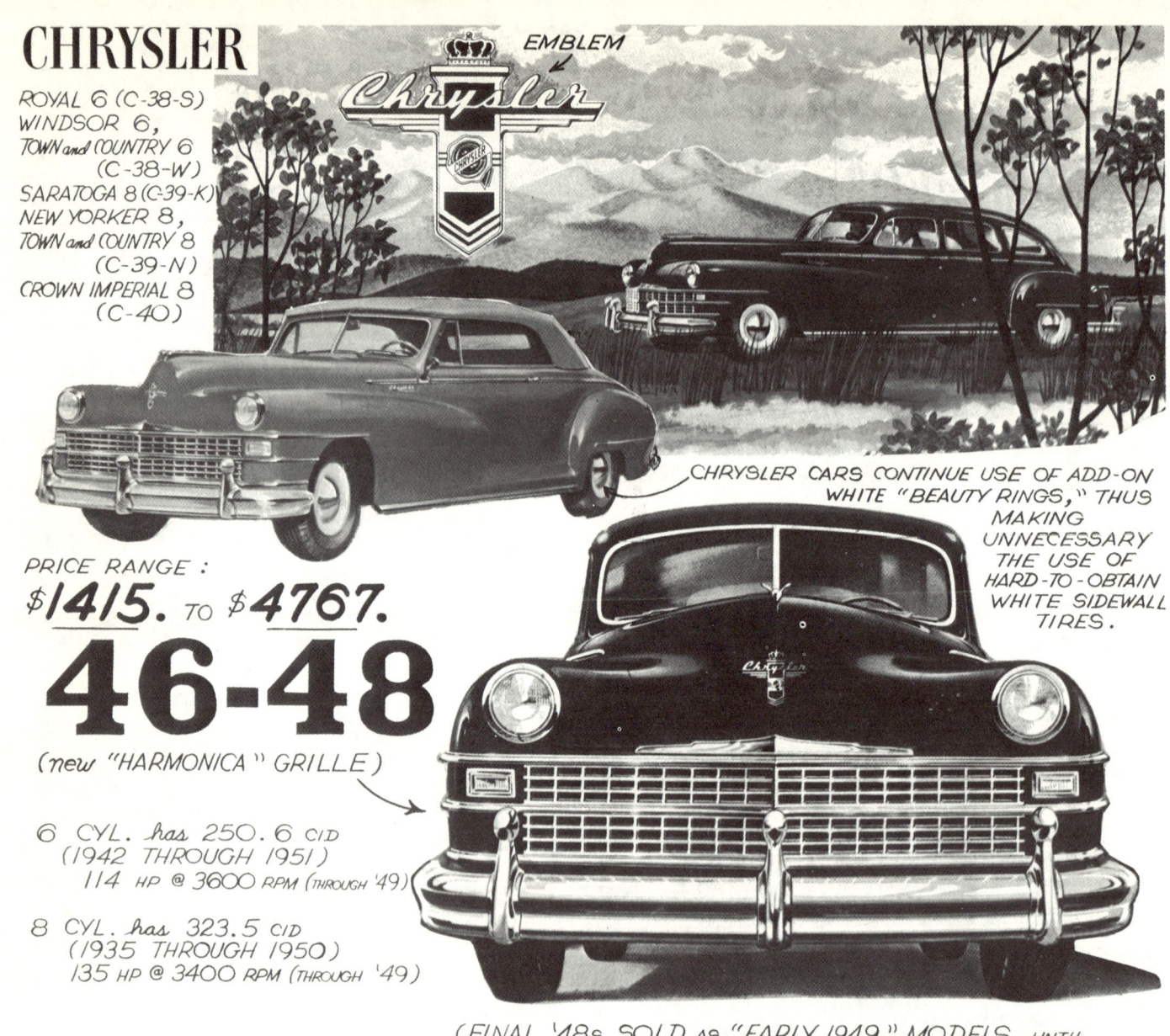

46-48

(new "HARMONICA" GRILLE)

6 CYL. has 250.6 CID
 (1942 THROUGH 1951)
 114 HP @ 3600 RPM (THROUGH '49)

8 CYL. has 323.5 CID
 (1935 THROUGH 1950)
 135 HP @ 3400 RPM (THROUGH '49)

(FINAL '48s SOLD as "EARLY 1949" MODELS, UNTIL RESTYLED MODELS AVAIL. FEB., 1949.)

121½" WB (6)
127½" WB (8)
145½" WB (CROWN IMPERIAL 8, THROUGH '54)
139½" WB (6-CYL. 8-PASS., LIMO.)

CHRYSLER

TOWN + CNTRY. H/T (ONLY 7 BUILT)

CONVENTIONAL CONVERTIBLE INTERIOR →

46-48 (CONT'D.)

(T+C FASTBACK SEDANS ONLY, 1941-1942)

TOWN and COUNTRY

$3123. ('48)

ONE-OFF 2-DR. BROUGHAM (EXPERIMENTAL)

'46 - EARLY 1947 "TOWN and COUNTRY" MODELS have GENUINE WOODEN PANELS OF ASH and MAHOGANY. (DK. PANELS ON LATER MODELS ARE DECALS)

CHRYSLER

WINDSOR 6

(C-45) 125½" WB (THROUGH '54)

CLUB COUPE

NEW YORKER 8

(LENGTH EXAGGERATED)

$3206.

ACTUAL LENGTH

NEW YORKER 8

NEW YORKER 8
(C-46) 131½" WB (THROUGH '52)

49
(TOTALLY RESTYLED)

PRESTOMATIC FLUID DRIVE* TRANSMISSION
*gyrol Fluid Drive

PRICE RANGE:
$2114.
TO
$5334.

$3970.
TOWN and COUNTRY 8 CONVERTIBLE
(SAME SPECS. AS NEW YORKER)

CROWN IMPERIAL 8 LIMO.
(C-47)

86

CHRYSLER

(FINAL YEAR FOR CHRYSLER STRAIGHT-8.)

ROYAL 6, WINDSOR 6 (C-48)

SARATOGA 8, NEW YORKER 8, TOWN and COUNTRY 8 (C-49)

50

PRICE RANGE $2114. TO $5334.

TOWN and CNT. 8 AVAIL. ONLY AS H/T.

new GRILLE →

NY 8 → NEW LOW LOOK! NEW LONG LOOK! NEW LOVELY LOOK!

$4003.

Crown Imperial

LIMOUSINE (C-50)

CRN. IMP. REAR COMP. has QUARTER WINDOWS.

8-CYL. MODELS NOW DEVELOP 135 HP @ 3200 RPM.

SARATOGA V8 (C-55) 125½" WB

NY V8 (C-52) 131½" WB

IMPERIAL V8 (C-54) (CRN. IMP. IS C-53)

WINDSOR 6 (C-51-1)

new WIN. DLX. 8 IS C-51-2

new 331.1 CID O.H.V. V8 REPLACES STRAIGHT 8 (180 HP @ 4000 RPM) (THROUGH '53.)

51

(CVT.) IS PACE CAR AT 1951 INDY 500 RACE

K-310 CUSTOM-BUILT COUPE

CHRYSLER

CUSTM BLT.

125 ½" W.B.
(ITALIAN GHIA BODY)
(WINDSOR 6 ENG. CHANGES FROM 250.6 TO 264.5 CID, 116 TO 119 HP @ 3600.)

PHAETON 147½" W.B.
(FOR PARADE USE, ETC.)

Imperial

BY CHRYSLER

A VARIETY OF ROSE WAS NAMED "CHRYSLER IMPERIAL."

IMPERIAL V8
(C-54)

52
(SIMILAR IN MOST RESPECTS TO 1951.)

(C-53)

CROWN IMPERIAL LIMOUSINE

$6994.

CHRYSLER WINDSOR 6 (C-60-1) WINDSOR 6

WINDSOR DELUXE 6 (C-60-2)

ALL EXCEPT IMPERIAL have 125½" WB (THROUGH '54)

$2555. UP

NEW YORKER V8 (C-56-1)

NY

(NEW YORKER DELUXE V8 IS C-56-2) (new)

53 (new 1-PIECE WINDSHIELDS)

CUSTOM IMPERIAL V8 (C-58) new 133½" WB

CROWN IMPERIAL V8 (C-59)

Imperial BY CHRYSLER

↑ IMPERIAL (STYLIZED EAGLE) HOOD ORNAMENT (new)

FOR 1954 TO 1965 IMPERIALS, SEE: IMPERIAL

89

CHRYSLER

WINDSOR DELUXE 6 (C-62) 264.5 CID, 119 HP @ 3600 RPM

NEWPORT H/T — $2831.

WINDSOR DELUXE TOWN and COUNTRY WAGON 6 $3321.

NY 331.5 CID V8s have 195 or 235 HP @ 4400 RPM

NEW YORKER (C-63-1)

NEW YORKER DELUXE (note small extra horizontal chrome piece on rear fender)

54 (FINAL 6-CYL.) DASH

NEW YORKER DELUXE V8 (C-63-2) SEE ALSO "IMPERIAL" SECTION

WINDSOR DELUXE (C-67)

ALL CHRYSLERS 126" WB, NOW V8-POWERED.
WINDSOR DLX. V8 has 301 CID, 188 HP @ 4400 RPM.

55 (RESTYLED)

TOWN and COUNTRY

NEW YORKER DE LUXE (C-68) (331 CID, 250 HP @ 4600 RPM)

$4109. — new **300** (C-300) 331 CID
300 HP @ 5200 RPM, 126" WB

90

CHRYSLER

New Pushbutton PowerFlite!
(Illustrated at right)

WINDSOR NEWPORT

DASH

(C-71) WINDSOR

56
126" WB

(C-72) NEW YORKER

N.Y. TOWN and COUNTRY

331 CID OR new 354 CID V8
(225 HP @ 4400; 250 or 280 @ 4600)

NEW YORKER GRILLE NOW DIFFERENT FROM OTHERS.

NEW PowerStyle **CHRYSLER FOR 1956**

(C-72-300) 300-B

NEW YORKER INTRODUCES VERTICAL CHROME STRIPS ON REAR FENDER (THROUGH '62.)

354 CID V8 (340 or 355 HP @ 5200)

91

CHRYSLER

57 (TOTALLY RESTYLED)

2-DR. H/T

WND. and SAR. have 354 CID V8 (285 or 295 HP @ 4600)

SEDAN $3088.

WINDSOR (C-75-1)

WINDSOR TOWN and COUNTRY WAGON

4 HEADLIGHTS on MOST MODELS

4-DR. H/T

(C-75-2) SARATOGA

SEDAN — note ONLY 2 HEADLTS.

(C-76) NEW YORKER 2 DR. H/T

4-DR. H/T

NEW YORKER has new 392 CID V8 (325 HP @ 4600 RPM)

$4259.

300-C has new HIGH and NARROWER GRILLE, also new 392 CID V8 (9.25 or 10 COMPR.) TWO 4-BBL. CARBS.

300-C ENGINE 375 HP @ 5200 or 390 HP @ 5400 RPM

H/T

300-C (C-76-300)

CVT. $5359.

THE MIGHTY CHRYSLER **300/C**

America's Most Powerful Car!

92

CHRYSLER

300-D (LC3-S)
380 OR 390 HP @ 5200 RPM

WINDSOR (LC1-L)

58
126" WB (new SHORTER 122" WB ON WINDSOR)

EXTRA! Now available on all Chryslers and Imperials! AMAZING NEW **auto-pilot** ...the remarkable new device that patrols your speed—warns you when you go too fast—lets you cruise "accelerator-free"—saves gas.
ANOTHER CHRYSLER ENGINEERING EXCLUSIVE

WINDSOR has 290 HP @ 4600 RPM (354 CID)

WINDSOR DARTLINE
note DIFFERENT SIDE TRIM on '58½ "DARTLINE" (ABOVE)

NEW YORKER

SARATOGA (LC2-M)
310 HP @ 4600 RPM (354 CID)

NEW YORKER (LC3-H)
345 HP @ 4600 RPM (SAME SIZE V8 [392 CID] as 300-D)

new ENGINES: 383 OR 413 CID

59 MC SERIES

305, 325, 350 HP @ 4600, OR 380 HP @ 5000 RPM

MORE 1959 CHRYSLERS ON NEXT PAGE

93

CHRYSLER

(MC2-M) SARATOGA

(MC1-L) WINDSOR

LION-HEARTED CHRYSLER '59

59 (CONT'D.)

(MC3-H) NEW YORKER

N.Y. TOWN and COUNTRY WAGON

CHRYSLER 300 (REAR FENDER BAND)
The international classic ...made in America

300-E (MC3-H)

$5749.

300-E

94

CHRYSLER 60

SARATOGA (PC2-M) has 383 CID V8 (325 HP @ 4600 RPM)

4-DR. H/T

WINDSOR CVT. has 383 CID V8 (305 HP @ 4600 RPM)

SAR. SEDAN

SARATOGA has GRILLE LIKE WINDSOR (ABOVE)

NEW YORKER (PC-3-H) has 413 CID V8 (350 HP @ 4600 RPM)

NEW PUSHBUTTON DASH PUTS ALL THE CONTROLS AT YOUR FINGERTIPS

NEW YORKER TOWN and COUNTRY WAGON

WINDSOR T+C

WNDSR.

NY CVT.

300/F BY CHRYSLER

The 300F medallion is molded like a gear wheel to express the rugged spirit of the car.

The open grille gives the 300F a "Pure automobile" look.

413 CID V8 (375 HP @ 5000 OR 400 HP @ 5200 RPM) (300-F)

(PC3-H)

95

CHRYSLER
wagon

(RC2-M) FINAL 1961 WINDSOR MODEL

$3303.

new NEWPORT LOW-PRICED SERIES 122" WB (RC1-L)

$3025. (NPT. H/T)

61

new GRILLES, CANTED HEADLIGHTS

NEWPORT has new 361 CID V8 (265 HP @ 4400 RPM) (OPTIONAL 413 CID V8 has 350 HP @ 4600 RPM)

413 CID V8 with 350 HP @ 4600 RPM IN RC3-H NEW YORKER

NY TOWN and COUNTRY

(FRONT END OF 300-G ILLUSTR. ON NEXT PAGE)

NY

$4133.

NEW YORKER SEDAN

96

CHRYSLER

300-G (RC4-P) has SAME ENGINES AS IN 1960

FINAL YR. OF 126" WB FOR 300 SERIES

61 (CONT'D.) →

300-G new GRILLE CLOSE-UP

62

NEWPORT

(SC1-2) NEWPORT

361, 383, 413 OR new 426 CID V8 ENGINES

300

265 HP @ 4400 RPM TO 421 HP @ 5400 RPM

300-H (SC2-M)

N.Y. 4-DR. H/T

N.Y.

ALL 122" WB (EXCEPT NY)

126" WB

NEW YORKER (SC3-H)

97

CHRYSLER

PAINTED IN ACRYLIC ENAMELS

ALL MODELS NOW have 122" WB. (THROUGH '64)

NEWPORT (TC1-L)

ROUND TAIL-LIGHTS IN 1963.

63 TC SERIES

(RESTYLED IN new "KNIFE-EDGE" [CREASE] BODY DESIGN.)

SAME 4 V8 SIZES AS IN 1962, BUT TOP "300" HP FIGURE NOW IS 425 @ 5600, with new TOP 13.5 COMP.

PACE CAR AT 1963 INDY 500 RACE IS 300-J.

DASH

← SALON (INTRO. 2-14-63)

NY TOWN and COUNTRY

(TC3-H) 1963 NEW YORKERS have VERTICAL LOUVRES ON FRONT FENDERS.

NEW YORKER

CHROME BANDS JOIN ENDS OF GRILLE WITH EDGES OF HOOD. (NY and 300)

300

NEW YORKER

(TC2-M) 300

CHRYSLER

VC1 SERIES 64

6 or 9-PASS.

Chrysler Newport — Hardtop Town & Country Wagon

NEWPORT

Chrysler Newport Convertible (VC1-L)

COMPRESSION RATIOS NOW RUN FROM 9.0 to 10.1 to 1.

361, 383 or 413 cid V8s (265 HP @ 4400 RPM to 290 HP @ 4800)

NEW YORKER (VC1-H)

NY SALON

VINYL TRIM ON ROOF

note GRILLE and SIDE TRIM VARIATIONS BETWEEN "300" CVT. and H/T MODELS ILLUSTRATED

WAGON

300 (K)

300 (VC1-M)

INTERIOR 300

99

Chrysler Newport Convertible (AC1-L) NEWPORT 7-W. SEDAN →

↑ 5-W. SEDAN

REAR INTERIOR (7-W. N.P. SEDAN)

NEWPORT CVT. (SHOWING DASH)

CHRYSLER MOTORS CORPORATION
CHRYSLER DIVISION

N.Y.

NEW YORKER (AC1-H)

65 AC1 SERIES

300-L

(AC1-M) 300-L's 413 CID V8 has SPECIAL CAM.
$4716. (CVT.)

'65's ONLY ENG. CHOICES ARE 383 OR 413 CID V8s (270 HP @ 4400 TO 360 @ 4800)

NEWPT. PRICES START AT **$3442.**

300 has LARGE RED CROSS IN CENTER OF GRILLE →

300 (AC1-M) **$4061.**

100

COMET (compact)

LINCOLN-MERCURY DIVISION — Ford Motor Company

(INTRO. 3-60)

FROM $1998.

60

6 CYL. OHV 114" WB 90 HP

two- and four-door wagons (109½" WB)

COMET

61

DASH SIMILAR TO 1960

new FRONT FENDER TRIM

new GRILLE

"Comet" NAME MOVED TO REAR FENDER

62

new ROUND TAIL-LIGHTS

NAME RETURNS TO FRONT FENDER

new GRILLE

CUSTOM

S-22

VILLAGER

101

Comet

63

COMET *SPORTSTER* hardtop

tach, bucket seats, Vinyl covered roof optional.

THE COMET CYCLONE. Super 289 cu. in. V-8, chrome engine parts, competition-type wheel covers.

(MIDSEASON MODEL)

64

DASH (CYCLONE)

CALIENTE

102

Comet

CYCLONE H/T

CALIENTE H/T

404

65

VILLAGER

202

REAR FENDER DETAIL

40 days from Cape Horn to Fairbanks

Cord

STARTS 1963

(SHORTER 100" WB REPLICA OF ORIGINAL 1936-1937 CORD)

DASH

150-180 HP CORVAIR 6 ENGINE

MFD. BY GLENN PRAY, BROKEN ARROW, OKLA.

103

FIBERGLASS TYPE BODY OF "ROYALEX"

OTHERS SUBSEQUENTLY INVOLVED IN PRODUCING THESE REPLICAS.

corvair

GENERAL MOTORS
(1960 – 1969)
COMPACT CAR
by Chevrolet

$1984. and up

DASH

569 SEDAN

500
(NO CHROME BELT TRIM)

60

WITH THE ENGINE IN THE REAR

AIR-COOLED 6-CYL.
REAR ENGINE-TRANSAXLE UNIT
140 CID
80 HP @ 4400 RPM
6.50 x 13 TIRES 108" WB

700

CLUB COUPE and INTERIOR (727)

SEDAN

BACK SEAT FOLDS, FOR CARGO.

$2103.
(769 SEDAN)

104

corvair

500 CLUB COUPE

spunkier 145-cu.-in. air-cooled rear engine

700

700 INTERIOR

4-DOOR SEDANS

note UNIQUE WHEEL COVERS ON NEW MONZA

new OPTION. ELECTRIC HOT AIR HEATER

new CORVAIR MONZA CLUB COUPE and INTERIOR

61

2 new WAGON TYPES and 2 SUB-TYPES

CORVAIR GREENBRIER SPORTS WAGON

SWINGING SIDE DOORS 95" WB

$2651.

GREENBRIER (STD.)

$2331.

LAKEWOOD STATION WAGONS

700 (735)

LAKEWOOD 500 (535)

SMART, DURABLE INTERIORS—Shown here: the 700's rich fabric-vinyl upholstery, offered in three color-keyed choices. 500 all-vinyl interior also comes in three color-keyed blends. Check the push-button locks on rear doors.

700

105

ENGINE UNDER REAR FLOOR.

corvair

500

62

GREENBRIER

MONZA

MONZA WAGON (ABOVE)
(FINAL YEAR FOR THIS
"LAKEWOOD" STYLE WAGON.
GREENBRIER VAN-TYPE
WAGON AVAIL. THROUGH
1965.)

63

DASH (ALL BUT SPYDER)

new CORVAIR SPYDER (150 HP)

MONZA

106

corvair

STD. ENGINE RAISED TO 95 HP.

DASH

64

MONZA

MONZA SPYDER (ABOVE) has 150 HP.

$3008.
(667 CVT.)

← DASH has CIRCULAR GAUGES.

MONZA

500

This year, all the coupes and sedans have hardtop styling

FROM **$2281.** **65**

new LARGER BODIES

(ONLY MAJOR CORVAIR RESTYLING)

MONZA SPORT SEDAN

140 HP (CORSA IS new TOP OF LINE MODEL.)

New power choices, too. There's a new 140-hp engine that's standard in Corsa models and can be ordered for all others—and a 180-hp power plant that you can specify for your Corsa.

107

CORVETTE Sports Car by CHEVROLET

6-CYL. CHEVROLET ENGINE (TO '55)

STARTS 1953

$3512.

53

FIBERGLASS BODIES (ON **ALL**)

('54) SPEAR on SIDE EMBLEM NOW POINTS UP.

ILLUSTRATED with DETACHABLE TOP

54-55

FULL-LENGTH SIDE TRIM   V-8 ENGINE ALSO (1955)

PRICE CUT 1955 ('55)

---

new TOP

56-57

new SIDE TRIM

V-8s ONLY

$2900. ('56)

$3437. ('57)

102" WB 230 HP   DASH

4 HEADLIGHTS

58

new VENT LOUVRE GROUP ON TOP OF HOOD (1958 ONLY)

$3631.

new BUMPERS

59-60

$3872. (IN '60; $3 LESS THAN '59)

108

CORVETTE

61 — $4272. — new GRILLE

62 — $4375. — new 250 HP — new SIDE-SCOOP DESIGN

63 — $4589. — new "STINGRAY" — new SIDE-SCOOPS AGAIN — new GRILLE, CONCEALED HEADLIGHTS, new 98" WB

64 — $4627. — new 1-PC. BACKLIGHT

Corvette Sting Ray Sport Coupe in Riverside Red
Corvette Sting Ray Convertible in Saddle Tan

65 — $4723. / $4508. — 4-WHEEL DISC BRAKES — 327 CID V-8 has 250, 300, 350, 365 or 375 HP @ 5500 RPM — new VERTICAL LOUVRE DESIGN

425 HP 396 CID V8
1965½ CORVETTE "396"

109

CROSLEY (1939-1952)

MFD. IN MARION, IND.

POWEL CROSLEY, JR.

FOUNDER OF CROSLEY CORP. (KNOWN AFTER WW 2 AS CROSLEY MOTORS)

39-42

2-CYL. AIR-COOLED WAUKESHA ENGINE (THROUGH '42)

12 HP

PRICE CUT TO $299. IN 1941.

$412. IN 1942

80" WB
4.25 × 12 TIRES

CVT. (OTHER MODELS ALSO AVAIL.)

"a FINE car" new 4-CYL. WATER-COOLED "COBRA" (COPPER-BRAZED) STAMPED-BLOCK 44 CID ENGINE (26½ HP @ 5400 RPM)

new BODY SIDES COMBINE with FULL-LENGTH FENDERS

WAGON

CVT. $1035. ('47)

$931. = SEDAN ('47)

new GRILLE, BUILT-IN HEADLIGHTS ABOVE

(TOTALLY RESTYLED) 80" WB

47-48

(POSTWAR PRODUCTION RESUMES DURING JUNE, 1946)

PICKUP

CROSLEY SPORTS-UTILITY

PANEL DELIVERY

110

CROSLEY

NOW CROSLEY HAS THE NEW LOOK

48½
new GRILLE ON MID-YEAR "NEW LOOK" SERIES

FOR 1949, COPPER-BRAZED, 58-lb. STAMPED ENGINE REPLACED BY IMPROVED CAST-IRON VERSION (CIBA.)

49-50

new GRILLE, "SPEEDLINE" STYLING

SEDAN

new "HOTSHOT" SPORTS ROADSTER

new HYDRAULIC DISC BRAKES (BY GOODYEAR-HAWLEY)

CVT.

WAGON

new BENDIX 9" HYDRAULIC BRAKES

Crosley Hotshot

SUPER

51-52

new 2-BLADED GRILLE *with* CENTER "SPINNER"

DISCONTINUED DURING 1952

111

DART

Dodge Division of Chrysler Corporation

FULL-SIZED LOWER-PRICED new COMPANION TO DODGE

SENECA

PIONEER (STARTS 1960)

PHOENIX

$2283. UP

118" WB (WAGONS 122") (THROUGH '61)

60

- PD3 (6 CYL.)
- PD4 (V8)

225 CID SLANT 6 *has* 145 HP @ 4000 RPM
318, 361 and 383 CID V8 *have* 230, 255, 310, 325 or 330 HP.

THE DODGE DART IS PRICED MODEL FOR MODEL WITH OTHER LOW-PRICE CARS.

DODGE DART	CAR F	CAR P	CAR C
SENECA	Fairlane	Savoy	Biscayne
PIONEER	Fairlane 500	Belvedere	Bel Air
PHOENIX	Galaxie	Fury	Impala

WAGON with TAILGATE OPEN

New Economy Slant "6" Uses Exclusive Semi-Ram Intake Manifold!

New design features inclined block with new Equi-flow fuel induction, overhead valves, for greater fuel economy.

112

DART
145 HP 6-CYL. CONTINUES

SENECA STATION WAGON 6 OR V8, 6 PASSENGER

SENECA 4 DOOR SEDAN 6 OR V8

SENECA

PIONEER STATION WAGON 6 OR V8, 6 OR 9 PASSENGER

PIONEER 4 DOOR SEDAN 6 OR V8

PIONEER

RD3 (6 CYL.)
RD4 (V8)

61

PHOENIX 4 DOOR HARDTOP 6 OR V8

PHOENIX

318, 361, 383 and new 413 CID V8s (230 to 375 HP)

DART 330 2-DOOR HARDTOP 6 OR V8

DART 330 4-DOOR 6-PASSENGER WAGON 6 OR V8

DART 330 2-DOOR SEDAN 6 OR V8

new 116" WB ('62 ONLY)

DART 440 9-PASSENGER WAGON V8

SAME DISPL. AS '61
145 TO 380 HP

62 (TOTALLY RESTYLED)
SD SERIES

DART 440 CONVERTIBLE V8

MODELS

DART 6 ══ (SD1-L)
 "   " 330 (SD1-M)
 "   " 440 (SD1-H)
DART V8 ══ (SD2-L)
 "   " 330 (SD2-M)
 "   " 440 (SD2-H)

1962 IS FINAL YEAR THAT DART IS DODGE-SIZED.

113   **THE NEW LEAN BREED OF DODGE**

DART

63 TL1 SERIES (RESTYLED)

- SEDAN
- 170
- WAGON
- 2-DR.
- 270
- DASH
- 8.2 COMPR.
- CVT.
- GT
- H/T

WHEELBASE REDUCED AGAIN, TO 111" (106" WB ON WAGONS)

$2288. UP

ALL 1963 DARTS ARE 6-CYL.
170 CID 101 HP @ 4400 RPM
OR 225 CID 145 HP @ 4000 RPM

---

64 VL1 (6) VL2 (V8)

- H/T
- GT
- 170
- SEDAN

TWO SLANT SIXES AS IN '63
new 273 CID V8 (180 HP @ 4200)

(270 STILL AVAIL.)

---

65 AL1 (6) AL2 (V8)

ENGINES AS IN 1964

Dodge Dart 4-door station wagon. 2-seat model only. 6 and V8 power.

$2310. UP

Dodge Dart 2-door sedan. 6 and V8 power.

Dodge Dart 270 convertible. 6 and V8 power.

- 270
- GT

Dart GT 2-door hardtop.

DART, DART 270, DART GT MODELS

114

DAVIS

**DAVIS MOTOR CO.,
VAN NUYS, CALIF.**

4 CYL.   3-WHEELER

(NO CONNECTION with the
DAVIS CAR MFD. BEFORE 1930)

(1947–1949)

(17 BUILT)

---

4 CYL.
CONTINENTAL
ENGINE

63 HP

(FEW BUILT)

(1949)

DEL MAR

DEL MAR MOTORS, INC.
SAN DIEGO, CALIF.

---

100 HORSEPOWER
@ 3600 RPM
6 CYL.

DE SOTO

228.1 CID
(SINCE '37)

COACH

DASH

40
S-7

4-DOOR

DeSoto
AMERICA'S FAMILY CAR
De Luxe Coupe $845 | De Luxe Sedan $905

6.00 × 16 TIRES
122½" WHEELBASE

A PRODUCT OF THE
CHRYSLER CORPORATION

DASH

new "ROCKET" BODIES

CUSTOM

1941 DeSoto

DLX.

FLUID DRIVE with *Simplimatic* Transmission (OPT.)

41 S-8

121½" WB (THROUGH '48)

100 HP (6.5 COMPR.)
105 HP (6.8 COMPR.)

DE LUXE COUPE **$898**†

DESOTO APPROVED SERVICE PLYMOUTH

new 236.7 CID (THROUGH '50)
115 HP @ 3800 RPM

42-45 S-10

NEW AIRFOIL LIGHTS
OUT OF SIGHT EXCEPT AT NIGHT

PERSONALIZED INTERIORS

6.25 × 16 TIRES
(6.50 × 16 ON 139½" WB MODELS)

COLOR-MATCHED TO YOUR TASTE

CUSTOM

TOP DISTORTED IN ARTIST'S VIEW

(AN ACTUAL PHOTO ON NEXT PAGE)

(1942-45
(THIS IS ONLY SERIES with CONCEALED HEADLIGHTS.)

116

WARTIME DE SOTO PRODUCTION of PARTS, ASSEMBLIES FOR GEN. SHERMAN TANKS (ILLUSTRATED,) BOFORS ANTI-AIRCRAFT CANNON, MILITARY PLANES, ETC.

"Styled to Stand Out — Built to Stand Up!"

DeSoto

42-45 (CONT'D.)

ONLY 24,771 1942 DE SOTOS PRODUCED AUG., '41 TO JAN., '42.

(ACTUAL PHOTO OF 1942 MODEL)

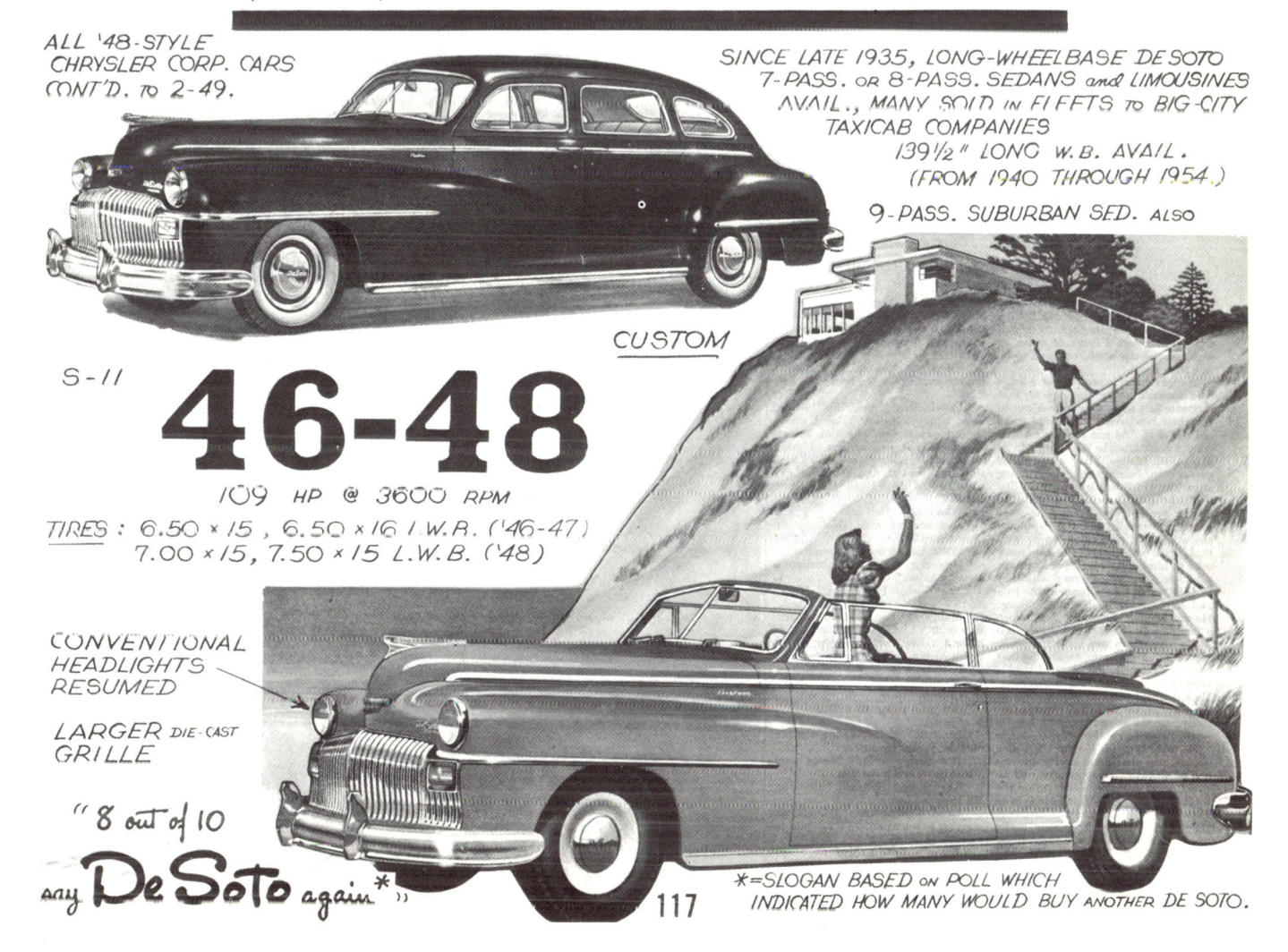

ALL '48-STYLE CHRYSLER CORP. CARS CONT'D. TO 2-49.

SINCE LATE 1935, LONG-WHEELBASE DE SOTO 7-PASS. OR 8-PASS. SEDANS and LIMOUSINES AVAIL., MANY SOLD IN FLEETS TO BIG-CITY TAXICAB COMPANIES
139½" LONG W.B. AVAIL.
(FROM 1940 THROUGH 1954.)
9-PASS. SUBURBAN SED. ALSO

CUSTOM

S-11

46-48

109 HP @ 3600 RPM
TIRES: 6.50 × 15, 6.50 × 16 I.W.B. ('46-47)
7.00 × 15, 7.50 × 15 L.W.B. ('48)

CONVENTIONAL HEADLIGHTS RESUMED

LARGER DIE-CAST GRILLE

"8 out of 10 say DeSoto again*"

*= SLOGAN BASED ON POLL WHICH INDICATED HOW MANY WOULD BUY ANOTHER DE SOTO.

De SOTO

DE LUXE
(has NO EXTRA CHROME FENDER STRIPS.)

CUSTOM

S-13 **49** (TOTALLY RESTYLED)

new 125½" WB (THROUGH '54)

CARRY-ALL SEDAN

112 HP @ 3600 RPM (THROUGH '50)

CLOSER VIEW OF 1949 GRILLE →

new SPORTSMAN H/T

RE-DESIGNED LIKENESS OF HERNANDO DE SOTO, HISTORIC SPANISH EXPLORER FOR WHOM CAR WAS NAMED

1950 GRILLE has PAINTED SECTION IN CENTER, with new EMBLEM.

new ROUND PARKING LIGHTS

S-14 **50**

Drive a De Soto before you decide!

DeSoto

SPORTSMAN H/T

S-15-1 (DE LUXE) S-15-2 (CUSTOM)

51

6-CYL. DISPLACEMENT RAISED TO 250.6 CID 116 HP @ 3600 RPM (THROUGH '54)

AS ON OTHER '51 CHRYSLER CORP. CARS, new "ORIFLOW" SHOCK ABSORBERS

new LOWER, SIMPLER GRILLE

1951 MODELS have SCRIPT LETTERING ABOVE GRILLE

new Full Power Steering

52

S-15 MODELS CONTINUE CUSTOM 6

1952 MODELS have BLOCK LETTERING ABOVE GRILLE

new FIRE DOME V8 (BELOW and RIGHT) (S-17)

S-17 CARS with AIR SCOOP HOOD ORNAMENT have new "FireDome" 276.1 CID V8 ENGINE

Power Braking

160 h.p. @ 4000 RPM

V-8

DESOTO-PLYMOUTH Dealers present GROUCHO MARX in "You Bet Your Life" every week

119

DeSoto

new MODEL NAMES

POWERMASTER 6
(S-18)

FIREDOME V8
(S-16)

V8
CONTINUES 276.1 CID
(THROUGH '54)

160 HP @ 4400 RPM

new POWER BRAKES and OVERDRIVE AVAILABLE

53

6 has a BROAD SHIELD EMBLEM on HOOD; V8 has "V" BELOW a NARROWER SHIELD (THROUGH '54)

SPORTSMAN

V8 has new 170 HP @ 4400 RPM

THE FINAL 6-CYL. DE SOTO

POWERMASTER 6
(S-20)

"POWERFLITE" A.T. AVAIL.

CORONADO SEDAN

FIREDOME V8
(S-19)

54

GRILLE MODIFIED new SIDE TRIM and TAIL-LIGHTS

DASH

DeSOTO — The *Forward* Look

new 126" WB

V8s ONLY (1955 ON)

FLITE-CONTROL gear selector lever is mounted on De Soto's smart, new instrument panel—out of your way. Yet at your finger tips.

(TOTALLY RESTYLED) 55

new 291 CID
FIREDOME (S-22) 185 HP @ 4400 RPM
FIREFLITE (S-21) 200 HP @ 4400 RPM

DRIVE A DE SOTO BEFORE YOU DECIDE

(PUSH-BUTTON A.T.)

DASH (MINOR CHANGES FROM 1955)

230 HP @ 4400 RPM
FIREDOME (S-23)

new 341.4 CID
ADVENTURER (S-24) 320 HP @ 5200 RPM

"HIWAY HI-FI" BLT.-IN RECORD PLAYER AVAIL.

new MESH GRILLE

TRIPLE TAIL-LIGHTS with OVERLAPPING FIN

new 330 CID

56

255 HP @ 4400 RPM
FIREFLITE (S-24)

PACE CAR AT 1956 INDY 500 RACE

new 12-VOLT ELEC. SYS.

DeSoto

new LOWER PRICE FIRESWEEP (S-27)
(has OWN FRONT END STYLING)

4-DR. H/T

(S-25) FIREDOME

SEDAN

new 325, 341 or 345 CID

245, 270, 295 or 345 HP

(TOTALLY RESTYLED) **57**

2-DR. H/T

FIREFLITE (S-26)

ADVENTURER
(4 HEADLIGHTS, ANODIZED GOLD TRIM)
(S-26)

new 122" WB on FIRESWEEP; 126" on OTHERS (THROUGH '59)

4-DR. H/T

EXPLORER WAGON (3 SEATS)

SHOPPER (2 SEATS)

FIREFLITE SEDAN

122

De Soto

16 MODELS, 4 SER.

new "TURBOFLASH" V8
(350 or 361 CID)

280 TO 355 HP

(LS2-M) FIREDOME

(LS1-L) FIRESWEEP

FIREFLITE (LS3-H)

CLOSE-UP **58** LS SERIES

LARGE new "CONTROL TOWER" WINDSHIELD

DASH

(LS3-S) ADVENTURER has ANODIZED SIDE TRIM

DE SOTO — the exciting look and feel of the future!

123

'59 DE SOTO

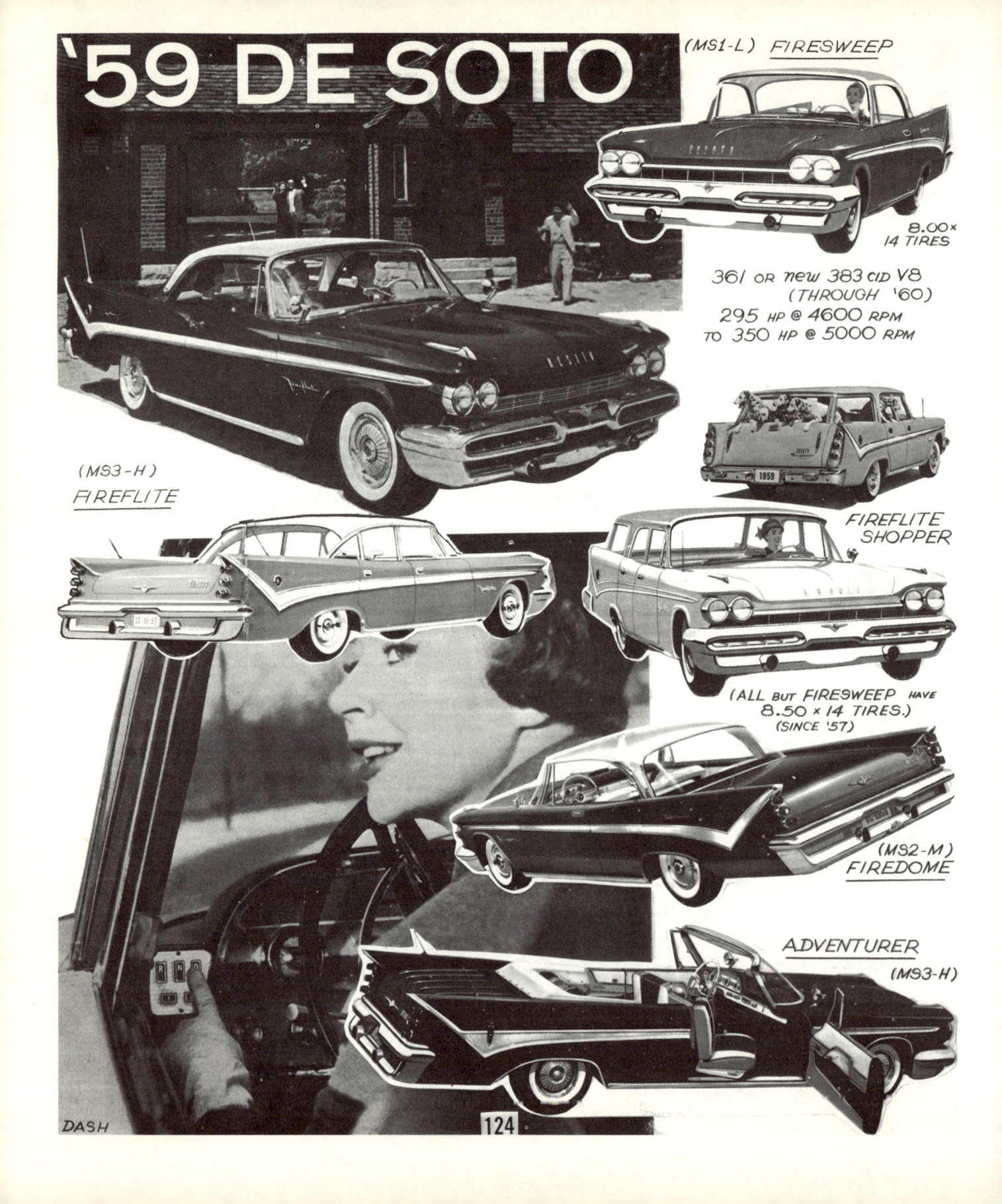

(MS1-L) FIRESWEEP

8.00 x 14 TIRES

361 OR new 383 CID V8
(THROUGH '60)
295 HP @ 4600 RPM
TO 350 HP @ 5000 RPM

(MS3-H) FIREFLITE

FIREFLITE SHOPPER

(ALL BUT FIRESWEEP HAVE 8.50 x 14 TIRES.)
(SINCE '57)

(MS2-M) FIREDOME

ADVENTURER (MS3-H)

DASH
124

1960 DE SOTO

DASH (with RAISED INSTRUMENT CLUSTER)

(PS1-L) FIREFLITE

(PS3-M) ADVENTURER

BUILT-IN 45-RPM RECORD PLAYER OPTIONAL AGAIN (AS IN PLYMOUTH)

H.P. CHOICES:
295 @ 4600; 305 @ 4600;
325 @ 4600 OR
330 @ 4800 RPM

10.0 TO 1 COMPRESSION

ALL 1960 and 1961 DE SOTOS ON 122" WB and 8.00 × 14 TIRES

1961 DE SOTO
ITS QUALITY SETS IT APART, ITS PRICE KEEPS IT WITHIN YOUR REACH

FROM $3102.

(THE FINAL DE SOTO CAR, AVAILABLE ONLY IN 2-DR. OR 4-DR. H/T BODIES)

4-DR. H/T

2-DR. H/T

ONLY THE 361 CID V8 IS AVAILABLE, with COMPRESSION REDUCED TO 9.0

265 HP @ 4400 RPM

ODD "SHARK-NOSE" TAIL-LIGHTS

PRODUCED 8-60 TO 12-60

DASH

The highly unusual instrument cluster. With the free type clock below the speedometer center. Not all options are shown.

2-TIERED GRILLE

DISCONTINUED

125

DODGE DIVISION · CHRYSLER CORPORATION · **DODGE** (EST. LATE 1914)

LUXURY LINER DE LUXE **$825** and up

1940 Dodge 2-door Sedan $815, delivered in Detroit

new 119½" WB (THROUGH '48)

DASH

40 D-17 = SPECIAL
D-14 = DE LUXE

87 HP @ 3600 RPM (SINCE '34)

3-WINDOW BUSNS. COUPE (new)

Slogan: "DODGE ENGINEERING COSTS NOTHING EXTRA" ('40)

FLUID DRIVE TRANSMISSION AVAIL.

6 CYL.

217.8 CID (SINCE '34)

91 HP @ 3800 RPM

D-19S = DELUXE
D-19C = CUSTOM

41 (RESTYLED)

DODGE SEDANS **$815** AND UP
COUPES, $755 and up

new LARGE, WIDE GRILLE

HOOD FOLDS "BUTTERFLY" STYLE

new Safety-Rim WHEELS

INTERIOR

126

DODGE

new 230.2 CID (TO '54)

new 6.7 COMPR. 105 HP @ 3600 RPM

new GRILLE with VEE CENTER SECTION

"THE NEW and the FINEST DODGE"

D-22S = DELUXE
D-22C = CUSTOM

42-45

7-WINDOW SEDAN

DASH and INTERIOR VIEWS

new 7.10 x 15 TIRES IN 1948

D-24S = DE LUXE
D-24C = CUSTOM

46-48

102 HP @ 3600 RPM

5-WINDOW SEDAN (ALL DOORS FRONT-HINGED)

"FADEAWAY" FENDERS

Dodge

SMOOTHEST CAR "AFLOAT"

127

ROADSTER (new) (TOP UP)

3-WINDOW COUPE

2-DOOR

(ACTUAL PHOTO) (TOP DOWN)

LOWER PRICED NEW DODGE *WAYFARER*

The Daring New DODGE
gyrol Fluid Drive plus GYRO-MATIC
Frees You from Shifting
OPTIONAL ON CORONET MODELS

49

D-29 = WAYFARER (115" WB)

D-30 = MEADOWBROOK and CORONET (123½" WB)

(SAME WBs THROUGH '52)

(ABOVE) WAYFARER ROADSTER (ARTIST'S CONCEPTION)

New Dodge CORONET

CORONET WAGON

103 HP @ 3600 RPM (TO '53)

new SWITCH KEY STARTING

LONGER on the inside ... SHORTER outside!
WIDER on the inside ... NARROWER outside!
HIGHER on the inside ... LOWER outside!

DODGE

new DIPLOMAT H/T

WAYFARER ROADSTER

INTERIOR

BACK SEAT

SUPER-SIZE LUGGAGE COMPARTMENT!

50

D-33 = WAYFARER
D-34 = MEADOWBROOK ; CORONET

new GRILLE with FEWER and HEAVIER PIECES

129

DODGE

WAYFARER

DASH

FEATHER-TOUCH BRAKING!
Big Safe-Guard Hydraulic Brakes stop smoothly, surely, safely. Cyclebond linings, with their larger braking surface, last up to twice as long. New feather-touch parking brake holds securely on even steep grades... easily released with a twist of the wrist.

51

D-41 = WAYFARER

D-42 MEADOWBRK. CORONET

SHOWN IN SAN FRANCISCO, LOOKING EAST TOWARD OAKLAND.

CORONET

D-41 and D-42 SERIES CONTINUE with LITTLE CHANGE

CORONET SIERRA WAGON

new HUBCAPS

1952 SERIAL NOs. START AT:

WAYFARER	MEAD./CORONET
37175001 (Detroit)	31867601
48009901 (San Leandro)	45090601
48507601 (Los Angeles)	
45527501 MD., COR., (L.A.)	

LOWER PART OF GRILLE is PAINTED.

52

CORONET "DIPLOMAT" H/T

FINAL YEAR FOR WAYFARER MODEL; REPLACED IN '53 BY MEADOWBROOK SPECIAL

DODGE

MEADOWBROOK 6
D-46

MEADOWBROOK SEDAN
MDBK. V8 is D-47

D-48 (114" WB)
D-44 (119")
CORONET V8

new 241.3 CID V8 (THROUGH '54)
140 HP @ 4400 RPM

Sensational New
140 Horsepower RED RAM V-8 ENGINE!

INTERIOR

CORONET SEDAN

6 OR V8

53
(RESTYLED)

WIRE WHEELS, CONTINENTAL SPARE AVAIL.

ABOUT 56% OF 1953 DODGES SOLD WERE V8s.

CORONET H/T

V8 MODELS have
DODGE V EIGHT
BELOW RAM HOOD ORNAMENT

114" OR 119" WB
(THROUGH '54)

131

DODGE

CORONET 6

6-CYL. NOW HAS 110 HP @ 3600 RPM

D-51, D-52 (6 CYL.)

54 D-50, D-53 (V8)

new GRILLE ROYAL V8

ROYAL 500 CVT. IS PACE CAR AT 1954 INDY 500 RACE.

H/T

ROYAL V8 SEDAN

V8 has 140 or 150 HP @ 4400 RPM (7.1 OR 7.5 COMPR.)

VARIOUS INTERIORS (JACQUARD FABRICS)

DEPENDABLE NEW '54 **DODGE** *Elegance in Action*

Fully-automatic PowerFlite and full-time Power Steering—yours at moderate extra cost.

DODGE FLASHES AHEAD IN '55

CORONET

REAR

CORONET V-8 2-DOOR SUBURBAN

ROYAL V-8 4-DOOR 8-PASSENGER SIERRA

V8 ENGINE NOW 270 CID

CUSTOM ROYAL V-8 4-DOOR SEDAN

new 3-TONE PAINT JOBS AVAIL.

55
D-56 (6 CYL.) (123 HP @ 3600 RPM)

H/T new CUSTOM ROYAL LANCER

D-55 (V8) (175, 183 OR 193 HP @ 4400)

CUSTOM ROYAL LANCER SEDAN

THE FORWARD LOOK ▶

new 120" WB (ON ALL, THROUGH '56)

6 CYL. NOW HAS 131 HP @ 3800 RPM (230 CID)
V8 has 189 TO 340 HP
(270, 315 OR 354 CID)

D-62 (6 CYL.)
D-63 (V8)

56

new FINS and EMBLEM IN GRILLE
new SIDE TRIM
DIPS AT REAR
new BUMPERS
HIGHER REAR FENDERS

The look, the feel, the power of success: New '56 Dodge Custom Royal Lancer 4-Door

In all the world no car like this
The New Dodge Lancer goes 4 door!

MORE 1956 DODGES ON NEXT PAGE

133

New '56 DODGE (CONT'D.)

VALUE LEADER OF THE FORW[ARD LOOK]

SIERRA

CORONET LANCER

ROYAL

CORONET

DASH

8-PASS. CUSTOM SIERRA

CUSTOM ROYAL CONVERTIBLE

$2121. UP

PUSHBUTTON POWERFLITE, greatest advance in driving ease and control. Proven by years of successful testing!

new TYPES OF PUSH-BUTTON TRANSMISSION CONTROL

CUSTOM ROYAL LANCER

REAR CLOSE-UP

134

'57 Dodge

SWEPT·WING (TOTALLY RESTYLED)
D-72 (6)   D-66, 67, 70 (V8)

new 325 or 354 CID V8s

2-DR. SUBURBAN (D-70)

CORONET (6 or V8) (D-72 or D-66)

4-DR. SIERRA (D-70) (D-71 is CUSTOM SIERRA)

ROYAL LANCER (D-67-1) 2-DR. H/T

CUSTOM ROYAL LANCER (D-67-2)

new 7.50 x 14 TIRES (8.00 x 14 WAGON, CVT.)

138 TO 340 HP

new 122" WB (ON ALL MODELS, THROUGH '59)

ADDED LOWER "TEETH" IN GRILLE of ABOVE LATER MODEL.

REAR FINS "OVERLAP" FENDER

new COMPOUND-CURVED WINDSHIELD

ROYAL

138 TO 333 HP
'325, 350 or 361 CID V8s

CORONET

CUSTOM ROYAL LANCER

EARLY 1958 MODELS ABOVE

LD-1 (6)
LD-2, LD-3 (V8)

58

SPRING SWEPT·WING by *Dodge*

58½ MODEL with IDENTIFYING CHARACTERISTICS

PAINTED HEADLIGHT AREA, also new GRILLE MEDALLION ON 58½

new colors   new interiors

135

'59 DODGE

Coronet 2-Door Sedan, V-8 or "6"

FINAL L-HEAD
230 CID 6
REDUCED TO 135 HP
@ 3600 RPM

59½
Silver Challenger
two-door sedan

SIERRA

326, 361 OR 383 CID V8s
have 255 HP @ 4400 RPM
TO 345 HP @ 5000 RPM

6 or V8

CUSTOM ROYAL

new TAIL-LIGHTS

SWIVEL-SEATS AVAIL. (new)

INTERIOR (CUSTOM ROYAL CVT.)

59
MD1-L (6)
MD2-L,
MD3-M,
MD3-L,
MD3-H (V8)

PUSH-BUTTON SHIFT PLAN

DASH

136

'60 DODGE

new O.H.V. SLANTED 6-CYL. ENGINE AVAIL. ONLY IN *new* SUBSIDIARY DART.

122" WB ON LARGE DODGES (THROUGH '61)

← MATADOR • POLARA →

361 OR 383 CID V8s (THR.'61) IN ALL DODGES EXCEPT *new* DART OR '61-2 LANCER

(295 OR 330 HP)

POLARA has BRIGHTWORK ON LOWER REAR FENDER.

PD1 and PD2 SERIES

new DART LISTED SEPERATELY

60

POLARA has HEAVY BAND ATOP FENDER

UNIBODY CONSTRUCTION

137

DODGE

61

265 TO 330 HP
122" WB

DASH — POLARA 2 DOOR HARDTOP V8

POLARA CONVERTIBLE V8

POLARA HARDTOP WAGON V8, 6 OR 9 PASSENGER

POLARA V8 IS ONLY LARGE SERIES

SEE ALSO DART, OR LANCER

62

Dodge Polara 500–2-dr Hardtop
Dodge Polara 500–4-dr Hardtop

POLARA 500

POLARA 500
361 OR 413 CID V8
305 OR 380 HP

(SD2-P) POLARA MODELS TOTALLY RESTYLED 116" WB (AS ON DART)

CUSTOM 880 (CONSERVATIVE OLDER TYPE STYLING) 122" WB
(SD3-L)
361 CID V8
265 HP @ 4400 RPM

138

1963 DODGE

330 SERIES

440 SERIES

116" OR 119" WB

225 CID 6 (145 HP @ 4000)

318, 383 OR 426 CID V8
(230 TO 425 HP)

POLARA SERIES

DASH

POLARA 500 SERIES BUCKET SEAT

TD SERIES 63

CUSTOM 880
361 OR 383 CID V8
(265 OR 305 HP)

122" WB

REAR VIEW OF CUSTOM 880 WAGON

139

'64 Dodge

225 CID 6 OR 318, 383 OR 426 CID V8

330

440 (VD-2) 7.00 × 14 TIRES

POLARA

SPORTSMAN WAGON

145 TO 425 HP

POLARA DASH — A-PARK.LOCK ; B-TRANSMISSION BUTTONS ; C-SPEEDO. ; D-CLOCK ; E-HEATER CONTROLS ; G-RADIO ; H-GLOVE BOX ; I-ASHTRAY, LIGHTER ; J-IGNITION ; K-WIPER CONTROL ; L-LIGHTS ; M-PARK.BRAKE RELEASE

note THAT POLARA DASH (ABOVE) DIFFERS FROM 880 DASH (see 880 CVT., BELOW)

880 WAGON

CONCAVE GRILLE ON 880

WRAPAROUND TAIL LIGHTS ON 880 (VA-3)

8.00 × 14 TIRES

880

'64 FINAL YR. OF '61-STYLE ROOFLINE ON 880

140

Dodge

AW1 (6) AW2 (V8)

Coronet

116" and 117" WB

Coronet

7.35 × 14 TIRES

Dodge Coronet 440 2-door hardtop. 6 and V8 power.

CORONET DASH

Dodge Coronet 440 Station Wagon (3-seat model also offered)

7.75 × 14 TIRES

145, 180, 230, 265, 270, 315, 330, 340, 365 or 425 HP.

Polara 4-door hardtop. V8 power. (AD2-L)

V-8 CHOICES INCLUDE 273, 318, 361, 383, 413 OR 426 CID

new 121" WB

Monaco two-door hardtop.

Dodge Monaco. Limited edition. 2-door hardtop. V8 power.

65 Monaco (AD2-P)

MONACO DASH

8.25 × 14 TIRES

Dodge Custom 880 4-Door Hardtop

Custom 880

880 (AD2-H)

Wagon has 8.50 × 14 TIRES

141

EDSEL $2519. UP

MFD. BY FORD MOTOR CO.
(1958, 1959, 1960 MODELS ONLY)

ROUNDUP 2-DR. WAGON

WAGONS HAVE SPECIAL TAIL-LIGHTS

note "HORSECOLLAR" CENTER GRILLE

"Teletouch" AUTO. TRANS. CONTROL BUTTONS IN STEERING-WHEEL HUB. (OPTIONAL) (1958 ONLY)

SLOGAN: "THIS IS THE EDSEL" (OTHER SLOGANS ALSO)

58

DASH → (with REVOLVING SPEEDOMETER)

VILLAGER 4-DR. WAGON

V-8s
361 CID, 303 HP
or 410 CID, 345 HP

BERMUDA 4-DR. (DELUXE WAGON with WOODGRAIN)

RANGER (LOWEST-PRICED)
(has MINIMUM of SIDE CHROME)

CITATION

CITATION (TOP OF LINE, has INSET PANEL SET WITHIN REAR FENDER TRIM LOOP.

PACER

CORSAIR

W.B.s:
116" (WAGONS)
118" (RANGER, PACER)
124" (CORSAIR, CITATION)

142

EDSEL

RANGER

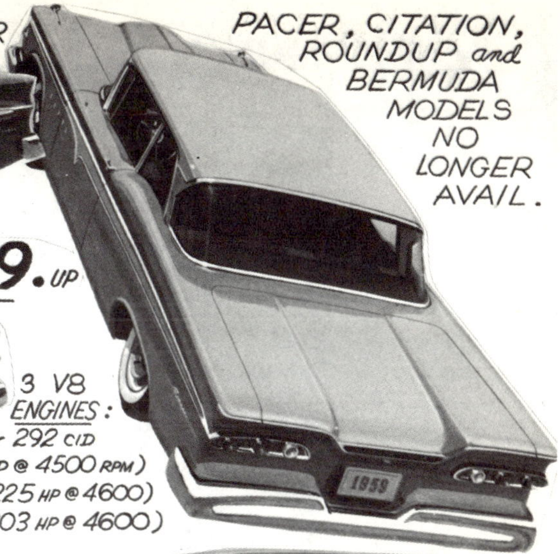

PACER, CITATION, ROUNDUP and BERMUDA MODELS NO LONGER AVAIL.

$2629.UP

223 CID 6-CYL. ENGINE ALSO AVAIL. STARTING 1959. (145 HP @ 4200 RPM)

3 V8 ENGINES:
Ranger 292 CID (200 HP @ 4500 RPM)
Express 332 CID (225 HP @ 4600)
OR Super Express 361 CID (303 HP @ 4600)

CORSAIR

new ROUND TAIL-LIGHTS

VILLAGER

new DASH

CORSAIR CHROME has VERTICAL STRIPS

59

SLOGAN: "MAKES HISTORY BY MAKING SENSE"

(RESTYLED)

INSET ANODIZED TRIM PANEL IDENTIFIES 1959 CORSAIR.

new 120" W.B. (ALL MODELS, THROUGH '60)

new GRILLE INCORPORATES HEADLIGHTS, with HORIZONTAL MEMBERS IN CENTER SECTION.

EDSEL

SLOGAN: "NEW! NIFTY! THRIFTY!"

CORSAIR NO LONGER AVAIL.

RANGER and VILLAGER ARE ONLY MODELS OFFERED FOR EDSEL'S BRIEF 1960 SEASON.

1960 MODEL PROD.:
WAGON, 6-PASS. (216)
WAGON, 9-PASS. (59)
2-DR. SEDAN (777)
4-DR. SEDAN (1,288)
2-DR. HARDTOP (295)
4-DR. HARDTOP (135)
CONVERTIBLE (76)
TOTAL = ONLY 2,846
1960 EDSELS BUILT!

60 (TOTALLY RESTYLED)

new TAIL-LIGHTS PICK UP VERTICAL OVAL THEME FORMERLY DISPLAYED IN EDSEL GRILLE.

FROM $2635.³⁰

RANGER

new SPLIT GRILLE

VILLAGER

new DASH

EDSELS DISCONTINUED NOV., 1959

3 ENGINE CHOICES:
Economy 6 223 CID
 (145 HP @ 4000 RPM)

Ranger V8 292 CID
 (185 HP @ 4200 RPM)

Super Express V8 352 CID
 (300 HP @ 4600 RPM)

FAIRLANE BY (FORD)

new COMPACT/INTERMEDIATE 6 OR V-8 for 1962; FORMERLY A FULL-SIZED FORD SERIES

62 $2392. UP

500 new CONCAVE GRILLE

63

SQUIRE

63½ AVAIL. with new VINYL ROOF

H/T INTERIOR

145

FAIRLANE

"289" V-8 option

Fairlane wagons:

FAIRLANE CUSTOM RANCH WAGON

64

SEE ALSO: **FORD**

optional features. 4-speed stick. Overdrive. Tachometer.

271 solid-lifter horsepower high-shift *automatic!*

$2474. UP

HEADLIGHTS PAIRED IN PLATES

NO MORE RAISED "AIR SCOOP" EFFECT ON HOOD

65

new OBLONG TAIL-LIGHTS

146

FALCON (compact) $1912. and up (1960 – 1970½ MODELS)
BY FORD
60

CHOICE OF 2-DR. OR 4-DR. WAGONS

109½" WB
6.00 × 13 TIRES

6 CYL. 144 CID
OVERHEAD VALVE ENGINE
90 HP

Ford MOTOR COMPANY

A CHOICE OF TWO SURGING "SIXES"!
STD. 144 CID OR new 170 CID

4-DR.
85 HP (STD.)

2-DR.

4-DR. WAGON ALSO AVAIL.
FALCON TUDOR WAGON

FORD *Falcon* '61
WORLD'S MOST SUCCESSFUL NEW CAR

new FUTURA CONSOLE

Futura

$2202. up

FUTURA has 3 DARTS on REAR FENDERS, and SPECIAL HUBCAPS.

Falcon '62
BEST SHAPE ECONOMY'S EVER BEEN IN

FUTURA

FALCON SPORTS FUTURA

FUTURAS HAVE SPECIAL FRONT FENDER TRIM, AS ILLUSTRATED.

DELUXE 2-DR.

4-DR.

DELUXE

new SQUIRE

STD. 2-DR.

63

STD.

new 164 HP V8 ALSO AVAIL.

FUTURA

DE LUXE

SQUIRE

new CONVERTIBLE

148

FALCON Lively new Sprint

THESE MODELS INTRODUCED IN MID-SEASON

63½

new scatback hardtop

Squire

new wider tread

64 (RESTYLED) $2211. UP
new '260' cu. in. V-8 power option

new longer springs

Squire

New battery-saving alternator.

65

13" OR 14" WHEELS

new 170 cu. in. standard Six with optional 3-speed Cruise-O-Matic transmission

new GRILLE

DASH

149

(SINCE 1903)

Ford

FORD Division of **FORD MOTOR COMPANY**

V8 L-HEAD ENGINE (SINCE 1932)

STANDARD has VERTICAL BARS IN NARROW GRILLE

DE LUXE

112" WB

1940 STANDARD GRILLE SOMEWHAT RESEMBLES THAT OF 1939 DE LUXE

4-PASS. COUPE has 2 FACING BACK SEATS

40

60 OR 85 HP (SINCE '37)

WITH 22 IMPORTANT IMPROVEMENTS

PRICES START AT $650. (STD. CPE.)

"STEP UP TO THE V·8 CLASS"

FINGER-TIP GEARSHIFT on steering post. All models, no extra cost.

new GRILLE

new SEALED-BEAM LIGHTS

TRANSVERSE SPRINGS CONTINUE (THROUGH '48 MODEL)

DE LUXE

FORD "Get the facts and you'll get a FORD!"

TUDOR SEDAN

CVT.

new 90 HP V8
new L-HEAD 6 also

41
(RESTYLED)

NEW Massive Beauty
NEW Room Throughout
NEW Vision All Around
NEW Faster Acceleration
NEW Stronger, Rigid Frame
NEW Longer Wheelbase
NEW Longer Springbase
NEW Soft, Slower-action Springs
NEW Soft Seat Cushions
NEW Stabilizer Ride Control

MODELS
SPECIAL (REPLACES STANDARD.
DELUXE
SUPER DELUXE

FORDOR SEDAN

PRICES START AT
$665. (V8 OR 6 SPECIAL CPE.)

new GRILLE

new 114" WB
6.00 x 16 TIRES

SUPER DE LUXE
FORDOR SEDAN

V8 OR 6 $780.
(SPECIAL 6 CPE.)
new RECTANGULAR PARKING LIGHTS

Steel Stampings for Die-Castings

42-45
"America's Most Modern 6...America's Lowest-priced 8"

Plastics Replace Metal for Interior Trim

DASH

new BROAD, LOW GRILLE with CURVED VERTICAL PCS.
"V8" OR "6" ON new EMBLEM

$930.

151

FORD PRICES START AT $1003. (6 CPE.)

V8 Six

NEW OVERSIZED BRAKES (on DRUMS)

CLUB COUPE

TUDOR FORDOR

There's a Ford in your future

46 1946 MODEL STARTS JULY, 1945

new GRILLE

NEW 1946 FORD SPORTSMAN'S CONVERTIBLE (V8) (with GENUINE WOODEN BODY)

$1865.

Outside and inside, there never was a car like this before! The new Ford Sportsman's Convertible is really *two* cars in one! Ford designers have combined the paneled smartness of the station wagon and the touch-a-button convenience of the convertible!

ALL METAL CVT. MORE COMMONLY SEEN (ILLUSTR. ON NEXT PAGE)

152

FORD

EARLY 47
(SIMILAR TO 1946)

Ford's out Front
(1947 SLOGAN)

CONVERTIBLE (METAL)

47½ - 48

1948 has new STEERING COLUMN LOCK.

...new stainless steel body molding newly fashioned door handles...

...new body colors...

$1517.* V8 WAGON

*= RAISED TO $1955 IN '48

There's a FINER *Ford* in your future

A newly styled instrument panel with big new dials for easy reading

new HOOD MEDALLION IDENTIFIES 6 OR V8

MODIFIED GRILLE NO LONGER has RED INDENTATIONS.

new ROUND PARKING LIGHTS PLACED BELOW HEADLIGHTS

new wheel rims and hub caps

new heavier bumper guards—And many other new features!

153

FORD

COUPE — PRICES START AT **$1333.** (DLX. COUPE) (6 CYL.)

TUDOR

CVT.

FORDOR

NEW! '49
STARTS SPRING, '48
(TOTALLY RESTYLED)

Overdrive
Engine speed 42 m.p.h. — Car speed 60 m.p.h.
(OPTIONAL)

57% more luggage space.

Wagon

new "Hydra-Coil" FRONT SPRINGS

(new CUSTOM SERIES REPLACES SUPER DE LUXE)

"6" OR "8" IN GRILLE "SPINNER" INDICATES NUMBER OF CYLINDERS.

CHOICE OF COLOR
Hard Tops
1. BLACK
2. COLONY BLUE
3. BAYVIEW BLUE
4. SEA MIST GREEN
5. ARABIAN GREEN
6. MIDLAND MAROON
7. BIRCH GREY
8. GUNMETAL GREY
Convertibles
9. FEZ RED
10. MIAMI CREAM

New "Flight Panel" dash...

154

FORD

"Country Squire" STATION WAGON

"Double Duty"

(8-PASS.

CVT.

50

CHASSIS (V8)

new MID-SEASON 2-DR. "CRESTLINER"

new EMBL. FM ON HOOD (also on DECK LID)

"TEST DRIVE" A '50 FORD

THERE'S A Ford IN YOUR FUTURE WITH A FUTURE BUILT IN!

155

FORD

CRESTLINE

51

DUAL SPINNERS IN GRILLE

new **VICTORIA**

VICTORIA INTERIOR

SQUIRE

new DASH

You can pay more but you can't buy better!

VICTORIA H/T with WINDOWS OPEN

REAR (SEDAN)

1951

FORD

PRICES START AT $1526.

new MAINLINE (has LEAST AMOUNT OF CHROME TRIM)

COUNTRY SQUIRE 4-DOOR METAL WAGON has IMITATION MAHOGANY PANEL DECALS, FRAMED with REAL MAPLE or BIRCH TRIM.

new RANCH WAGON

new COUNTRY SEDAN

Station Wagons

52 (TOTALLY RESTYLED)

New Flight-Style Control Panel

Ford's new Center-Fill Fueling cuts down spillage.

CUSTOMLINE 2-DR.

DASH

new SUSPENDED PEDALS

"TEST DRIVE" A FORD TODAY — YOU CAN PAY MORE BUT YOU CAN'T BUY BETTER

HUGE, curved, one-piece windshield and car-wide rear window to match. You can really see what's ahead and what's behind!

CRESTLINE SUNLINER V8 CRESTLINE VICTORIA

new GRILLE has APPEARANCE of 3 "SPINNERS"

$2104.

Full-Circle Visibility

101 h.p. High-Compression Mileage Maker Six

"Only V-8 in its field!"

110 h.p. High-Compression Strato-Star V-8

157

FORD

CVT. IS PACE CAR AT 1953 INDY 500 RACE

PRICES START AT **$1537.**
(MAINLINE 6 CPE.)

MAINLINE 2-DR

DASH

FORD 50TH ANNIVERSARY

53

ONLY ONE "SPINNER" IN NEW GRILLE.

SUNLINER

FORD-O-MATIC (SINCE '51)

COUNTRY SQUIRE

2-DOOR RANCH WAGON **$2019.** (6)

4-DOOR COUNTRY SEDAN

158

Ford Skyliner (CRESTLINE SERIES)

COUNTRY SQUIRE

NO SHIFTING...NO CLUTCHING

$2199.
(V8 $134 EXTRA)
with PLEXIGLASS ROOF WINDOW

54

New 130-h.p. **Y-BLOCK V·8**

239 CID V8 ENDS '54

MAINLINE

New Ball-Joint Front Suspension

New 115-h.p. **II-BLOCK SIX**

223 CID (THR. '64)

4. Four-Way Power Seat.
UP / DOWN / FRONT AND BACK

CUSTOMLINE

5 optional power assists*

★ Master-Guide power steering does up to 75% of steering work... ★ Swift Sure Power Brakes do up to one-third of your stopping work... ★ Fordomatic Drive does *all* your shifting ... ★ Power-Lift Windows open and close at a button's touch. And ★ 4-Way Power Seat adjusts up or down, forward or back, at a touch of the controls.

*At extra cost

159

FORD

PRICES START AT **$1606.** (MAINLINE 6 CPE.)

SEDAN MAINLINE

new GRILLE

new FAIRLANE SUNLINER CVT. (ABOVE)

CUSTOMLINE

new "WRAP-AROUND" WINDSHIELD

120-H.P. 6 OR V8s with 162 OR 182 H.P.

55

RANCH WAGON

CUSTOM RANCH WAGON

6-PASS. COUNTRY SEDANS

COUNTRY SQUIRE

8-PASS. (with FAIRLANE SIDE TRIM)

"Y" SYMBOLIZES Y-BLOCK V8 new 272 CID

FAIRLANE VICTORIA

SIDE EMBLEM (ON FAIRLANE TYPES)

FAIRLANE CROWN VICTORIA (note BAND WRAPPED OVER ROOF)

new FAIRLANE MODELS IDENTIFIED BY SWEEP SIDE TRIM

160

FORD

V-8 h.p. upped

MAINLINE

6 NOW 137 HP @ 4200 RPM

CUSTOM RANCH WAG.

FAIRLANE FORDOR

The 272-cubic inch Ford V-8, the standard eight for all Customline and Mainline Fords. Has modern dual carburetor, automatic choke, single exhaust.

CTY. SQUIRE

The 292-cubic inch Thunderbird V-8, the standard eight for all Fairlanes and Station Wagons, is now available in all Customline and Mainline models, too. Has 4-barrel carburetor, dual exhausts.

202 H.P.

CUSTOM COUNTRY SEDAN

new 2-DR. LUXURY PARKLANE WAGON (INTRO. TO COMPETE with CHEVY's NOMAD.)

56

CUSTOMLINE VICTORIA

SKYLINER — CROWN VICTORIA

The 312 cubic inch Thunderbird Special V-8,

225 h.p.

new 4-DR. H/T (FAIRLANE FORDOR VICTORIA)

1956 INTERIOR

161

FORD

6 CYL. INCREASED to 144 HP

CNTRY. SED. SQUIRE

RANCH WAGON

CUSTOM TUDOR

CUSTOM 300 FORDOR

LADDER-TYPE CONTOURED FRAME

4-way ball-joint front suspension

CUSTOM (REPLACES MAINLINE)

FAIRLANE (note UNIQUE SIDE TRIM)

New deep-offset hypoid axle

FAIRLANE 500 MODELS BELOW

UP TO 245 HP with "SILVER ANNIVERSARY V8s."

57

FAIRLANE 500 4-DR. TOWN VICTORIA H/T

LOW-SILHOUETTE CARB.

new V8 SKYLINER has RETRACTABLE HARD TOP (POWER-OPERATED)

SUNLINER CVT.

$2942

new FRONT END

REAR

162

FORD
6 CYL. NOW 145 HP (THROUGH '60)
CUSTOM 300
FAIRLANE 500 SKYLINER (SHOWN with TOP IN MOTION, and with TOP IN PLACE.)
DASH
NOTHING NEWER IN THE WORLD
RANCH WAGON
(4-DR. ALSO AVAIL.)
DEL RIO RANCH WAGON
COUNTRY SEDAN
COUNTRY SQUIRE (2 VIEWS)
58
(TOTALLY RESTYLED)
NEW INTERCEPTOR V-8
PRECISION FUEL INDUCTION
A TRUE AIR RIDE
FINE-CAR DETAIL
new ROOF GROOVES
4 HEADLIGHTS
4 TAILLIGHTS
Versatile Cruise-O-Matic Drive! Set selector in D1 position for brisk, solid-feeling take-off. Select D2 for gentle, sure-footed starts. What's more, when new Cruise-O-Matic Drive is teamed with a new Interceptor V-8 engine it can give you up to 15 per cent more gasoline mileage.
V8s = 292, new 332 and new 352 CID (THROUGH '59)
F-1958
FAIRLANE 500
Up to 300 h.p. with new Precision Fuel Induction.

FORD

CUSTOM 300

$2132. (6)

note "FORD" LETTERING ON HOOD

WINDSHIELD DOGLEG DETAILS

Fairlane 500

FAIRLANE 500 VICTORIA ROOFLINE (CLOSE-UP)

note EMBLEM ON HOOD

new GRILLE

FAIRLANE REAR FENDER

(TOTALLY RESTYLED AGAIN)

59

145 TO 300 HP

NEW FORD GALAXIE CLUB VICTORIA—THUNDERBIRD STYLING IN A 6-PASSENGER, 2-DOOR HARDTOP

new 1959½ TOP-OF-LINE GALAXIE MODELS ADDED, with T-BIRD ROOFLINE.

THE FINAL SKYLINER (GALAXIE)

164

FORD wagons

ROOMY NEW FORD RANCH WAGON... LOWEST PRICED WAGON OF THE MOST POPULAR THREE

4-DOOR and 2-DOOR RANCH WAGONS

FENDER CHEVRONS ON THIS '59½ RANCH WAGON

(INTERIOR VIEW EXAGGERATED)

59 (CONT'D.)

COUNTRY SQUIRE
$3076*

1959 DASH (ILLUSTR. with FACTORY-INSTALLED AIR CONDITIONER UNIT)

*WAGON PRICE SHOWN APPLIES TO V-8 9-PASSENGER 6 CYL. or 6-PASS. MODELS also avail.

COUNTRY SEDAN
$2947.*

165

FORD

FAIRLANE 500

FAIRLANE PRICES START AT **$2170.** (6-CYL. 2-DR.)

GALAXIE TUDOR

(TOP UP)

SUNLINER CVT.

(TOP DOWN)

new STARLINER **$2723.** (V8; 6 ALSO AVAIL.)

ARCHED TAIL-LIGHTS ONLY ON 1960 MODELS →

GALAXIE FORDOR

NEW SLOPING HOOD GIVES INCREASED VISIBILITY

60 145 TO 300 HP (TOTALLY RESTYLED FOR 3RD SUCCESSIVE YEAR!)

DASH

RANCH WAGON

← COUNTRY SEDAN

9-passenger Country Squire

166

Beautifully built to take care of itself...

FORD '61

GALAXIE 4-DR. TOWN VICTORIA H/T

(CLOSER VIEW OF GALAXIE WHEEL COVER AT UPPER RIGHT)

SQUIRE

2-DR. FAIRLANE
FAIRLANE 500 (6 CUT TO 135 HP)
4-DR.
WHEEL COVER

new GRILLE IS CONCAVE, BISECTED HORIZONTALLY

$2261. (6)

RANCH WAGON

STATION WAGONS

CNTRY. SEDAN

292, 352 OR new 390 CID V8s (175 TO 401 HP)

GALAXIE VICTORIA H/T (CLOSE-UP and DASH)

STARLINER H/T

ROUND TAIL LIGHTS RETURN

1961

FORD

RANCH WAG.

COUNTRY SQUIRE

6-PASSENGER COUNTRY SEDAN
(9-pass. model also)

SLOGAN: **live it up with a lively One from FORD**

Galaxie 62

new BLUNTED REAR END

138 to 405 HP (THR. '63)

POWER STEERING

GALAXIE 500/XL. DENOTES 405 HP THUNDERBIRD ENGINE

GALAXIE 500 and XL have GRILLE MEDALLION

1962 TAIL LIGHTS

BUCKET SEATS and FLOOR CONSOLE in new Galaxie 500/XL!

new * SIDE TRIM

*= ON 500, XL

Galaxie 500 (SEDAN and CVT. ILLUSTR.)

168

FORD

GALAXIE

SQUIRE

new GRILLE with SHIELD EMBLEM, AND STEP-UP ALONG LOWER EDGE

63

new SIDE TRIM

note INDENTATION ALONG UPPER BORDER OF WOOD-LIKE "COUNTRY SQUIRE" SIDE TRIM.

BACKGROUND: MONACO, ON THE RIVIERA

DASH

PRICES START AT **$2563.**
6-CYL. "300" 2-DR.

UP TO 425 HP IN new '63½

new

Presenting the 63½ Super Torque Ford Sports Hardtop —brand new hardtop that looks like a convertible!

169

new SWING-AWAY STEERING WHEEL AVAILABLE

FORD

'64

- CLEAR GLASS BACKLIGHT IN CVT.
- CUSTOM RANCH WAGON
- SQUIRE
- 138 to 425 HP
- GALAXIE 500 4-DR. H/T
- GALAXIE 500 XL
- new GRILLE
- PRICES START AT $2586. (CUSTOM 6 2-DR.) ($2600 IN '65)

'65 (RESTYLED) 150 to 425 HP (THROUGH '67)

- new VERTICAL STACKED HEADLIGHTS
- CUSTOM 500
- new DIP IN WAGON ROOF
- Convenient face-to-face rear seats add passenger space
- SQUIRE
- GALAXIE 500 XL
- GALAXIE 500 LTD
- TAIL LIGHT SHAPE IS new

170

FRAZER

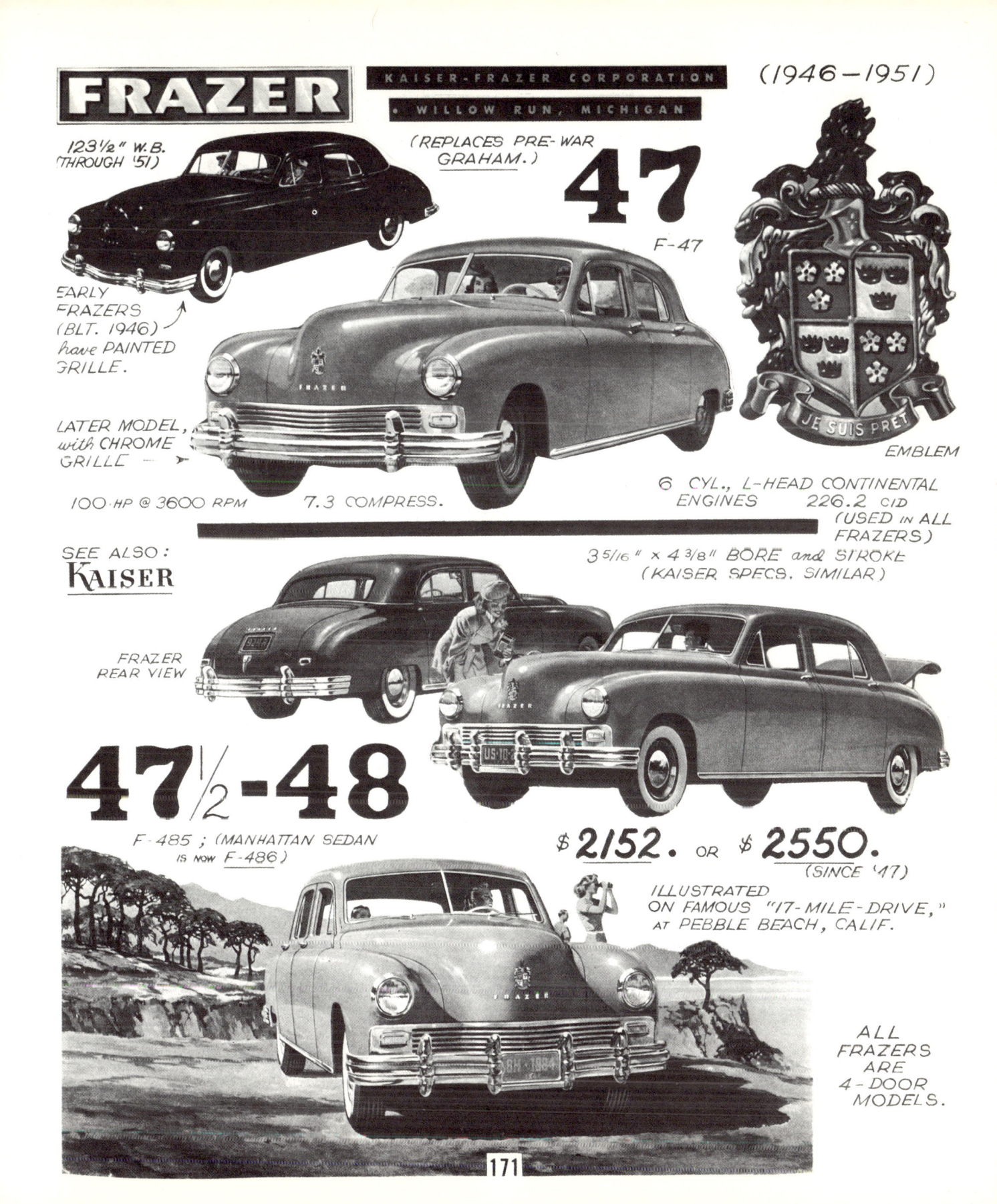

KAISER-FRAZER CORPORATION • WILLOW RUN, MICHIGAN

(1946-1951)

(REPLACES PRE-WAR GRAHAM.)

47
F-47

123½" W.B. (THROUGH '51)

EARLY FRAZERS (BLT. 1946) have PAINTED GRILLE.

LATER MODEL, with CHROME GRILLE →

100 HP @ 3600 RPM   7.3 COMPRESS.

6 CYL., L-HEAD CONTINENTAL ENGINES   226.2 CID (USED IN ALL FRAZERS)

3 5/16" x 4 3/8" BORE and STROKE (KAISER SPECS. SIMILAR)

EMBLEM — JE SUIS PRET

SEE ALSO: KAISER

FRAZER REAR VIEW

47½-48
F-485; (MANHATTAN SEDAN IS NOW F-486)

$2152. OR $2550. (SINCE '47)

ILLUSTRATED ON FAMOUS "17-MILE-DRIVE," AT PEBBLE BEACH, CALIF.

ALL FRAZERS ARE 4-DOOR MODELS.

171

FRAZER

48 (CONT'D.)

JOSEPH W. FRAZER (left) and HENRY J. KAISER (right,) STANDING BY THE 200,000th CAR (A 1948 FRAZER) TO BE BUILT BY THE KAISER-FRAZER CORP.

J.W. FRAZER — H.J. KAISER

49-50

112 HP

VAGABOND

PRICED FROM **$2321.**

F-505 and F-506 MANHATTAN are 1950 MODELS.

MANHATTAN SEDAN has HEAVY BAND of SIDE CHROME

1949 = F-495 OR F-496 MANHTN.

new LARGE GRILLE and PARKING LIGHTS

(1950 MODEL ENDS 2-50)

4-DOOR CVT.

new "MANHATTAN" LOOKS LIKE THE 4-DR. CVT., but has STEEL PAINTED OR NYLON-PADDED TOP SECTION.

VAGABOND

115 HP

51 (RESTYLED)

F-515 OR F-516 MANHATTAN

DASH (SIMILAR TO 1949)

STARTS 2-50

172

EXPERIMENTAL SAFETY CAR BLT. 1945 to 1947 BY
H. GORDON HANSEN,
AT SAN LORENZO, CALIF.

FORD V8 ENGINE

GORDON DIAMOND

156" WB BETWEEN FRONT REAR SINGLE WHEELS. ANOTHER PAIR OF WHEELS "AMIDSHIPS."
PURCHASED BY HARRAH'S AUTOMOBILE COLLECTION

GRAHAM (and HUPMOBILE)

6-CYL. L-HEAD ENGINES

115" WB

FORMER CORD BODY DIES USED

40-41

'41 GRAHAM: $895. and up
'40 HUPP: $1145. and up

GRAHAM "HOLLYWOOD" and HUPMOBILE "SKYLARK" LOOK ALMOST ALIKE!

(FURTHER DETAILS OF GRAHAM, HUPMOBILE INCLUDED IN "AMERICAN CAR SPOTTER'S GUIDE, 1920-1939")

GREGORY

(1949) (ANOTHER EXPER. MODEL, 1952)

BEN GREGORY, MFR., KANSAS CITY, MO.

4-CYL. Continental REAR ENGINE FRONT-WHEEL-DRIVE

49

PRODUCTION ATTEMPTED

40 HP 94" WB

$1050. (PROPOSED PRICE)

(1948-1949)

HOPPENSTAND

HOPPENSTAND MOTORS, INC., GREENVILLE, PA.

2-CYL. FLAT, AIR-COOLED, REAR ENG.

48-49

173

(1950-1954)

Henry J

PRICED FROM
$1299.
(WITH PERIODIC INCREASES)

4 OR 6-CYL. "SUPERSONIC" ENGINES

(2-DRS. ONLY)

THIS GRILLE STYLE RETAINED ON 1952 HENRY J

513 = 4 CYL.
514 = DELUXE 6 CYL.

51
(INTRO. 1950)

KAISER-FRAZER CORPORATION, WILLOW RUN, MICHIGAN

GIVEN THE FASHION ACADEMY GOLD MEDAL AWARD

52-54

('52) ALLSTATE CAR = SPECIAL SERIES OF HENRY J, SOLD EXCLUSIVELY BY SEARS, ROEBUCK and CO.

CORSAIR ('53-'54)

Henry J new GRILLE ON '53-54

new VAGABOND has REAR "CONTINENTAL" SPARE TIRE/WHEEL

Vagabond ('52)

174

HUDSON MOTOR CAR CO., DETROIT
SERIES (6-CYL.)
40 = TRAVELER; DELUXE (113" WB)
41 = SUPER (118" WB)
43 = COUNTRY CLUB (125" WB)
48 = BIG BOY (125" WB)

HUDSON SIX
(1909-1957)

$670 COUPE (6)

92 HP @ 4000 (174.9 CID 6) OR 102 HP @ 4000 (212 CID 6)

INTERIOR (6)

TOTAL OF 86,865 BLT.

new GRILLE

SERIES (8-CYL.)
44 = SUPER
45 = DELUXE (118" WB)
47 = COUNTRY CLUB (125" WB)

40

OVERDRIVE AVAIL.
4.11 STD. GEAR RATIO
6.50 × 16 TIRES

DASH →

H.P. RATINGS CONTINUE THROUGH '47

(CVT.) SUPER 8

128 HP @ 4200 **STRAIGHT 8** (254.5 CID 8)

SHOULD HYDRAULIC BRAKES FAIL, EMERGENCY MECHANICAL SYSTEM TAKES OVER (SINCE '36)

"AUTO-POISE" FRONT WHEEL CONTROL WITH COIL SPRINGS

INTERIOR (8)   NEW HUDSON EIGHT PRICES START AT **$860**

175

HUDSON
PRICES START AMONG AMERICA'S LOWEST
$695

79,529 BLT. 1941

SUPER 6 (SERIES 10)

"SYMPHONIC STYLING"

41

116", 121", OR 128" WB

"AMERICA'S SAFEST CAR"

new COMMODORE 8

• COMMODORE SERIES (Sixes and Eights)

ONLY 5,396 BLT. IN 1942

42-45

new EXTRA SIDE CHROME

COMMODORE 6 IS new

SUPER 6

CIVILIAN PROD. ENDS 2-5-42.

SOME '42s NO LONGER have FRONT HOOD CHROME

POSTWAR PRODUCTION RESUMES 8-30-45. 5,005 BLT. 1945; 93,870 BLT. 1946

SUPER 6

46

121" WB ON ALL (THROUGH '47) PRICED FROM $1379.

COMM. has 2 VERT. STRIPS on REAR WINDOW

new GRILLE with RECESSED CENTER SECTION

COMMODORE (has $1379. UP

HUDSON TRIANGLE EMBLEM AT FRONT END OF CHROME BELT STRIP)

PRICED FROM $1421.

SUPER 6

47

103,310 BLT. 1947

COMMODORE $1421. UP

SIMILAR TO 1946, BUT has HEAVIER CHROME MOULDING MARGIN AROUND MEDALLION OVER GRILLE.

HUDSON

CVTS. NOW HAVE MORE METAL ABOVE WINDSHIELD

142,454 BLT. 1948

new "Step Down" BODIES SURROUNDED BY FRAME

INTERIOR ('49)

48-49
(TOTALLY RESTYLED)

new 124" WB ON ALL

"This time it's Hudson"

50

new PACEMAKER 6 IS LOWER-PRICED SERIES (119" WB)

REAR SEAT VIEW

ROAD CLEARANCE

INVERTED "V" ON new GRILLE

COMMODORE 8

143,586 BLT. 1950

51

92,859 BLT. 1951

PACEMAKER 6
$2642.

SUPER 6

new HEAVIER, ARCHED GRILLE

COMM. 8
$2543.

$2568.

new **HORNET 6**

PACEMAKER 6

COMMODORE 6

HUDSON WASP TWO-DOOR BROUGHAM

CVT.

new **HUDSON WASP** with 6-CYL. "H-127" ENG.

Hollywood H/T (new)

HOLLYWOOD WASP

CLUB CPE.

HORNET CLUB CPE.

new lower-priced running mate

52
HUDSON HORNET

SEDAN

HORNET

HUDSON

equipped with
B-W OVERDRIVE!
(OPTIONAL)

B-W ENGINEERING PRODUCTION

79,117 BLT. 1952

HYDRA-MATIC DRIVE
available for all '52 Hudsons
at extra cost.

Hudson-Aire Hardtop Styling
at standard sedan and coupe prices

COMMODORE 8

FINAL YEAR FOR STRAIGHT 8

178

HUDSON SUPER WASP 1953: 17,792 WASPS, 27,208 HORNETS   HORNET

6-CYL. MODELS ONLY (THROUGH 1954)

new HOOD "AIR-SCOOP" and new GRILLE w/o INVERTED "V."

53

(The *JETS* SHOWN ON "JET" PAGE)

The **WASPS** in the low-medium price field

SUPER WASP

new HIGH TAIL-LIGHTS

HUDSON DIVISION OF AMERICAN MOTORS
(RESULT of MERGER with NASH, 5-1-54)

new 1-PC. WINDSHIELD

The **HORNET** in the medium price field

CLUB COUPES

new FRONT END DESIGN

54
(RESTYLED)

NEW HORNET SPECIAL
available in Four-Door Sedan, Club Sedan and Club Coupe—all at new low prices

2-DR. CLUB SEDAN

4-DR. SEDAN

HORNET has 160 HP

(170 HP with "Twin H" Power)

INTERIOR of HOLLYWOOD (CAR ILLUS. NEXT PAGE)

new CHROME PC. ON SIDE

179

HUDSON 54 (CONT'D.)

HORNET HOLLYWOOD H/T

32,293 HUDSON CARS BLT. 1954

52,688 BLT. 1955 ("HUDSON" NAME also USED on SOME Ramblers and Metropolitans)

CUSTOM WASP SEDAN

new ENGINE CHOICES

V8 CHAMPIONSHIP 6

55 (TOTALLY RESTYLED with NASH BODY DESIGN)

HOLLYWOOD H/T

PACKARD V8 USED

22,588 BLT. 1956

new PEAKS OVER HEADLIGHTS

BIG new DIAMOND-SHAPED GRILLE

56

HOLLYWOOD H/T

SEDAN   DASH

180

HUDSON

$2750.

HORNET SUPER

DASH with new Hydra-Matic

new SIDE TRIM MOULDINGS

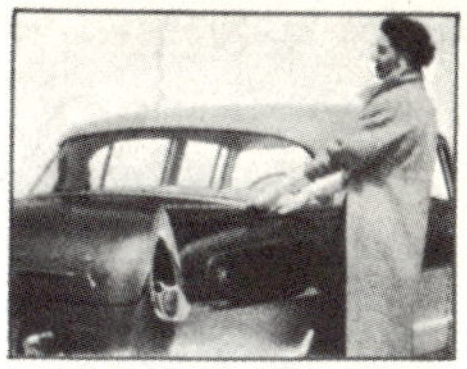

Hornet V-8

Lower outside by 2 full inches

327 CID — World's newest V-8 ... 255 hp

57 new "V" EMBLEM ON GRILLE

ONLY 4,080 BLT. 1957

IS ONLY AVAIL. MODEL (SUPER OR CUSTOM)

HORNET HOLLYWOOD H/T (APPEARS LONGER IN PHOTO AT LEFT THAN IN PHOTO ABOVE.)

(DISCONTINUED JUNE 25, 1957)

Slim outside for easy maneuvering

...way up in power, way down in price!

(1949-50)

IMP

INTERNATIONAL MOTOR PRODUCTS CO., GLENDALE, CALIF.

49-50

FIBERGLASS BODY
63" WB   APPR. 475 lbs.
1-CYL., 7-H.P. GLADDEN engine

SOME REPORTS LIST FINAL DATE AS 1955.

181

IMPERIAL

54

CUSTOM (C-64) 133½" WB

331.1 CID V8 (3 13/16 × 3 5/8)
235 HP @ 4400 RPM

(EARLIER MODELS ILLUSTRATED with CHRYSLER.)

CROWN (C-66) 145½" WB

7.5 COMPR. (SINCE '51)

55

new 331 CID V8 (3.81 × 3.63)
250 HP @ 4600 RPM

new 8.5 COMPRESSION

IMPERIAL (C-69) 130" WB

CROWN IMPERIAL (C-70) 149½" WB (THROUGH '56)

(IMPERIAL CONSIDERED AN INDIVIDUAL MAKE, AS OF 1955.)

56

IMPERIAL (C-73) new 133" WB

354 CID; 280 HP @ 4600 RPM

CROWN IMPERIAL (C-70)

IMPERIAL

(IMI-1) **$5598.** new 129" WB (THROUGH '66)

new 392 CID (THROUGH '58)
325 HP @ 4600 RPM
new 9.25 COMPR.

57

new 129" WB (THROUGH '66)

note DIFFERENCES IN NUMBER OF HEADLIGHTS

CROWN (IMI-2)

LE BARON (IMI-4) **$5743.**

LE BARON SOUTHAMPTON

new 10.0 COMPRESSION
345 HP @ 4600 RPM

FENDER-GRILLE DETAILS

LYI SERIES **$5969.**

58

IMPERIAL NAME (NON-LE BARONS)

IMPERIAL

CUSTOM SOUTHAMPTON (MY1-L)

59

LE BARON SOUTHAMPTON (MY1-H)

LE BARON

new CROWN (MY1-M)
413 CID, 10.1 COMPR. (THROUGH '65) 350 HP @ 4600 RPM (THROUGH 61) '65)

60

(PY2-M) CROWN

(PY1-L) CUSTOM SOUTHAMPTON

$4933. TO $6318. PRICE RANGE

CUSTOM 4-DOOR SOUTHAMPTON

new 8.20 x 15 TIRES (THROUGH '64)

(PY3-H) LE BARON

IMPERIAL

CROWN (RY1-M)

SOUTHAMPTON

new "FREE-STANDING HEADLIGHTS (THROUGH '63)

61

(RY1- SERIES)

America's Most Carefully Built Car

ORNAMENT at HOOD FRONT; new SPLIT GRILLE

IMPERIAL LE BARON 4-DR. SOUTHAMPTON (SY1-H)

CUSTOM is SY1-L

CROWN (SY1-M)

62

RAISED TAIL-LIGHTS

HP REDUCED TO 340 @ 4600 RPM (THROUGH '65)

4-DR. SOUTHAMPTON

185

IMPERIAL

CROWN (TYI-M)

WHEEL COVER

HIGH, NARROW TAIL-LIGHTS

DASH

(FINAL YEAR FOR "CUSTOM" SERIES.)

(TYI-L) CUSTOM

63

(TYI SERIES)

(HAND-BUFFED ACRYLIC ENAMELS)

(TYI-H)

IMPERIAL Le BARON

The LeBaron cloisonné crest on the roof makes this the only car on which this federal jewelry excise tax is paid.

FREE-STANDING HEADLIGHTS FOR 3RD AND FINAL YEAR

IMPERIAL

CROWN COUPE (VYI-M)

(VYI-M)

Imperial Crown 4-Door Hardtop

LE BARON (VYI-H)

DASH

(VYI SERIES) **64**
$5865. TO $6740.

(TOTALLY RESTYLED; new DESIGN SOMEWHAT RESEMBLES LINCOLN CONTINENTAL.)

EAGLE CREST ON LE BARON VINYL TOP →

AUTO PILOT (left)
AM/FM RADIO (above)

↘ HEADLIGHTS MOVED INTO new SPLIT GRILLE.

The Incomparable IMPERIAL

IMPERIAL CROWN COUPE (AY1-M)

CHOICES OF UPH. INCL. REAL LEATHER

65 DASH

LIGHT FLASHES IF FUEL, OIL, TEMP. GAUGES NEED ATTENTION.

AIR COND. DUCTS (ON DASH)

HEADLIGHTS PAIRED BEHIND GLASS PANELS.

new GRILLE

(LE BARON IS AY1-H)

188

INTERNATIONAL

Motor Truck Division
International Harvester Company
180 North Michigan Avenue Chicago 1, Illinois

INTERNATIONAL STATION WAGONS

(new "D" SERIES STARTS SPRING, 1937.)

39-40
"D" SERIES 6 CYL.

113" WB

See the New Green Diamond Engine

"K" LINE SERIES

41-46

47-49
"KB" SERIES

new OVERHEAD VALVE ENGINES (SILVER DIAMOND, SUPER BLUE DIAMOND, SUPER RED DIAMOND TYPES)

ALL-STEEL TRAVELALL WAGON

50-52

new GRILLE and 1-PIECE WINDSHIELD

('52)

INTERNATIONAL 53-55

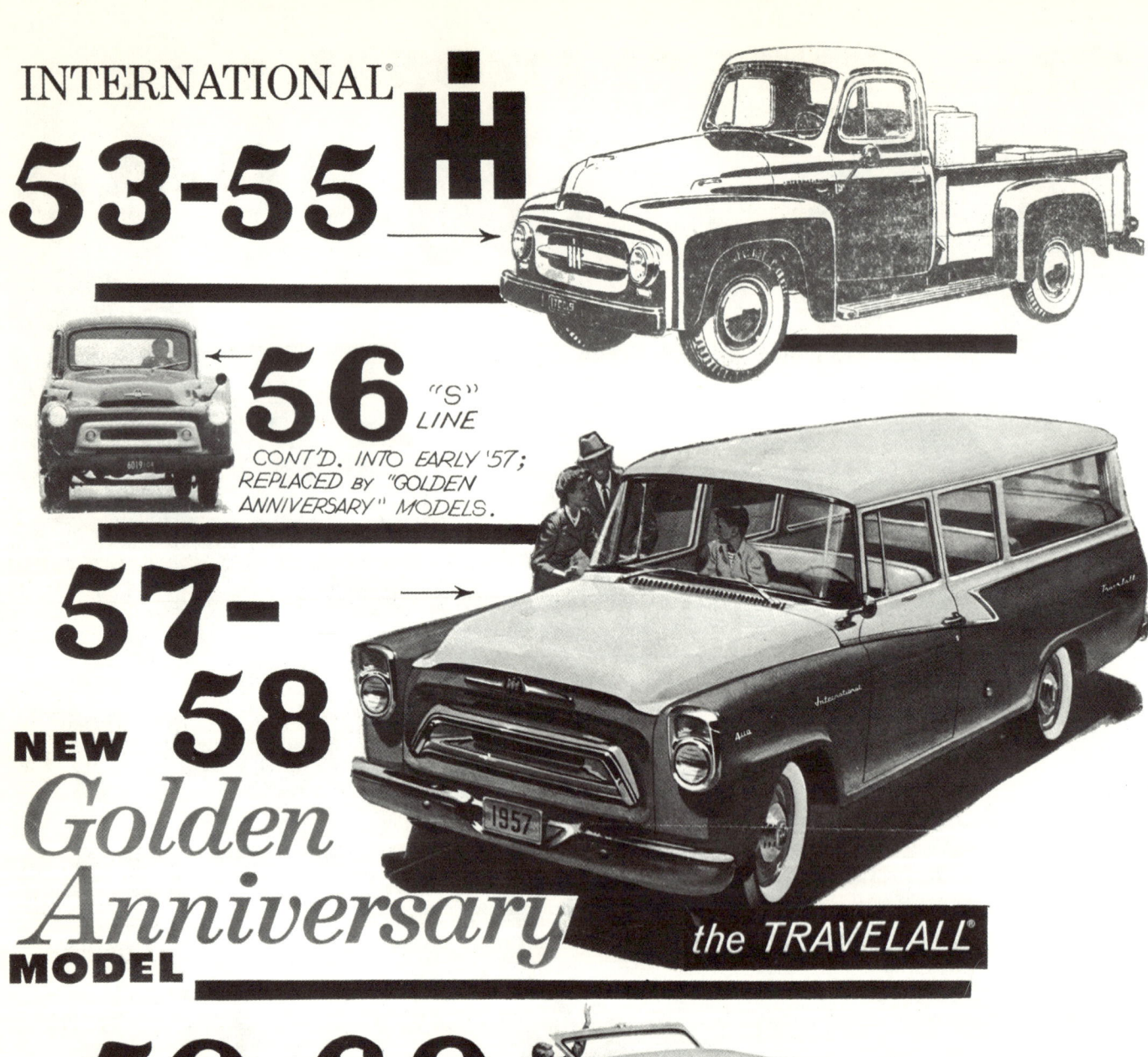

56 "S" LINE
CONT'D. INTO EARLY '57; REPLACED BY "GOLDEN ANNIVERSARY" MODELS.

57-58 NEW Golden Anniversary MODEL

the TRAVELALL

59-60

GRILLE (TRUCK)

The Travelall

INTERNATIONAL 61-62 Scout

The Travelall

SCOUT is *new* FOR 1961.

63-64

(SCOUT ALSO CONTINUES)

THE TRAVELALL

65

THE Scout BY INTERNATIONAL

191

JET (1953–1954)

53 — 22,089 JETS BLT. 1953 — $1858. and up — JET by HUDSON — 6 CYLS. — 104 HP

SUPER JET — DASH

105" WB

IN ALL THE WORLD NO OTHER CAR LIKE THIS!

54

JET — $1885.

5.90 x 15

SUPER-JET — $1933.

DASH — BUCKET SEATS

ITALIA (ONLY 26 BUILT, ON SUPER-JET CHASSIS)

JET-LINER — $2057.

note THAT EACH SERIES IS QUICKLY IDENTIFIED IN '54 BY AMOUNT OF CHROME SIDE TRIM.

SEE ALSO: **Hudson**

KAISER

KAISER-FRAZER CORPORATION • WILLOW RUN, MICHIGAN

(1946 – 1955)

EMBLEM

EARLY MODEL, BUILT 1946

KAISER SPECIAL — with CORRUGATED BUMPER

47
K-100 OR K-101 CUSTOM

KAISER 6 — with PLAIN BUMPER

SPECIAL = $1868.
CUSTOM = $2547.

AS IN FRAZER, 6-CYL., L-HEAD CONTINENTAL ENG. (ON ALL)
6.50 x 15" TIRES
123½" W.B.

47½ – 48
K-481 OR K-482 CUSTOM

$1967.
$2557.

SEE ALSO: *FRAZER*

ALL OVER THE MAP—YOU'LL FIND EXPERT KAISER AND FRAZER SERVICE

K-F Distributors and parts warehouses
K-F Dealers, parts and service stations

KAISER FACTORY-APPROVED PARTS AND SERVICE FRAZER

ILLUSTRATED AT CAPE COD, MASS.

new 7.10 x 15" TIRES

note 4 VERTICAL BUMPER GUARD ARRANGEMENT ('47½-'48 ONLY)

TRAVELER MODELS FEATURE FULL-OPENING REAR "HATCHBACK."

2-cars-in-one

$2088*
Kaiser Traveler
(new)

new 4-DOOR CONVERTIBLE

49-50

new 112 HP

"TRAVELER" MODEL NAME IN SCRIPT

SEDAN

REAR 3/4 VIEW OF VIRGINIAN

new GRILLE

new VIRGINIAN 4-DOOR HARDTOP

GEAR RATIOS: 4.09; 3.91; 3.73 (OR 4.27 with OVERDRIVE)

194

Kaiser

new 2-door sedan

SEE ALSO: "HENRY J"

new HORIZONTAL BLADE GRILLE

K-511 = SPECIAL
K-512 = DE LUXE

1951
(TOTALLY RESTYLED)

115 HP @ 3650 RPM

new HIGH, ARCHED TOP with HUGE WINDOW AREA

new 118½" WB

The newest car in America!
Anatomic Design*

(HOOD ORNAMENT ADDED (ON ALL))

new "GOLDEN DRAGON" (with "ALLIGATOR" TYPE UPH., etc.)

HUBCAP VARIATION

Hydra-Matic AUTO. TRANS. OPTIONAL (THROUGH '55; also OPT. on 1951 FRAZER)

Built to Better the Best on the Road!

MODELS
SPECIAL
VIRGINIAN
DE LUXE
MANHATTAN

'52 Kaiser *Manhattan*

new 1-PIECE WINDSHIELD

new BUMPER-BRIDGE PROTECTS 1952 GRILLE.

118 HP

PRICES START AT **$1992.**
(SPEC. COUPE)

Kaiser's Anatomic Engineering...

world's safest front seat!

1. Slant-back corner posts—narrower—no "blind spots"!
2. One-piece Safety-Mounted Windshield—designed to push *outward* upon severe impact!
3. Safety-Cushion Padded Instrument Panel!
4. Right hand emergency brake!
5. Recessed instruments—no protrusions!
6. Safety-level seat *balances* you more safely!
7. Extra front legroom—you sit in a *safer* position!

INTERIOR DETAILS

New

K-521 = VIRGINIAN SPECIAL ; DE LUXE
K-522 = VIRGINIAN DE LUXE ; MANHATTAN

KAISER

PRICED FROM $2313.

new "V" FIGURE ADDED TO LOWER PART OF FRONT and REAR EMBLEMS.

CAROLINA 2-DR. (K-538) (new)

REAR DETAILS

53

DE LUXE TRAVELER (K-531 IS DE LUXE SERIES)

118 HP
118½" WB

MANHATTAN (K-532)
(DRAGON IS K-530)

MERGES WITH WILLYS-OVERLAND, TO FORM KAISER-WILLYS.

(LENGTH EXAGGERATED)

OPTIONAL SUPERCHARGER GIVES 140 HP @ 3900 RPM (STD. HP 118) '55

KAISER-DARRIN DKF-161 WITH (fiberglass body)

$3668.
new LIGHTS and CONCAVE GRILLE

6 CYL
161 CID
WILLYS F-head ENGINE

('54)

'55 SIMILAR, BUT WITH HIGHER CHROME FIN TIP ON HOOD ORNAMENT (SEE ARROW)

54-55

1955 PRICES START AT $2503.

SIMILAR MODELS CONTINUED BY KAISER IN ARGENTINA (I.K.A.), UNDER THE NAME OF CARABELA. (1955 TO 1962.)

REAR ALSO RESTYLED

197

KING MIDGET

46-50

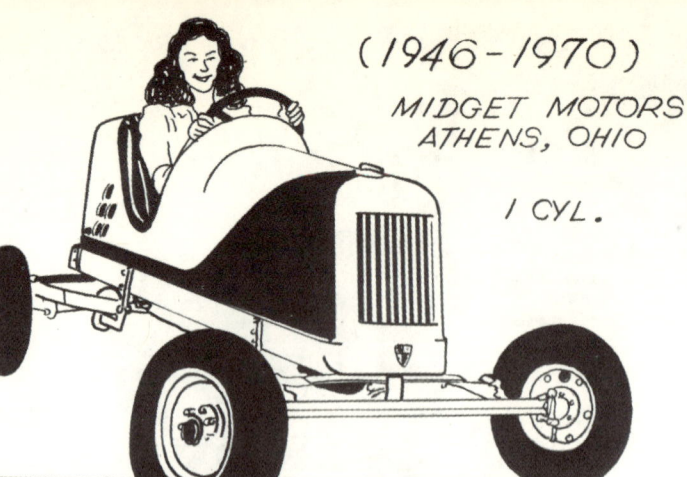

(1946-1970)
MIDGET MOTORS
ATHENS, OHIO

1 CYL.

EARLY 51-57

(TOTALLY RESTYLED FOR 1951)

('55)

LATER 57-70

(RESTYLED EARLY '57)

30% HP INCREASE (TO 12 HP) FOR 1966

KOHLER ENG.

DISCONTINUED 1970
$1095. IN '69

KURTIS

(1949-1950)
CHOICE OF V-8 ENGINES
100" WB

KURTIS-KRAFT, INC.
LOS ANGELES and GLENDALE, CALIF.
(FRANK KURTIS, founder)

KURTIS CONTINUED TO BUILD OTHER TYPES OF SPORTS and RACING CARS, AFTER EARL MUNTZ BEGAN PRODUCING "JET"*

* BECOMES MUNTZ JET IN '51, new 116" WB and ENLARGED TO 4-PASS.

LANCER [DODGE] COMPACT — CHRYSLER CORPORATION

Lancer 170 Two-Door Sedan — $2312.

WAGON

LARGER 225 CID 6 ALSO AVAIL., with 145 HP @ 4000 RPM OR 196 HP @ 5200 RPM

6 CYL. INCLINED O.H.V. ENGINE 170 CID with 101 HP @ 4400 RPM OR 148 HP @ 5200 RPM

61 RWI-L, RWI-H

AIR COND., POWER STEERING and POWER BRAKES AVAIL.

INTERIOR

106½" WB

LANCERS BUILT 1961 and 1962 ONLY. UNITIZED BODY SIMILAR TO PLYMOUTH VALIANT.

H/T COMPACT DODGE LANCER

LANCER 170 2-DOOR SEDAN 6 — $2256 (SLI-L)

LANCER 170 4-DOOR SEDAN 6

LANCER 770 4-DOOR SEDAN 6

LANCER 170 6-PASSENGER WAGON 6

LANCER 770 2-DOOR SEDAN 6

$2562. — new GT

62 SLI

770 (SLI-H) — 1962 new GRILLE

(SLI-P) DISCONTINUED AFTER 1962

LARK BY STUDEBAKER
COMPACT SERIES (1959-1963)

59

2-DR. PLAY WAGON

6-CYL. OR V8 ENGINES

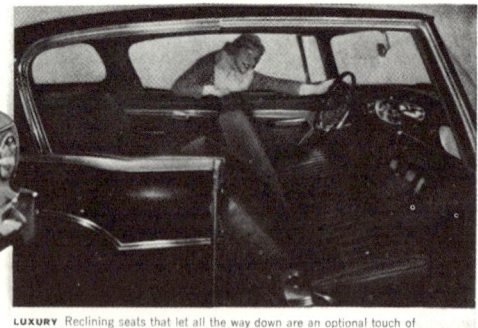

note LOCATION of GRILLE MEDALLION on 1959 MODEL

1959 LARK CARRIES "STUDEBAKER" NAME

LUXURY Reclining seats that let all the way down are an optional touch of sublime comfort. Seats are pleated, appointments tasteful. Colors are harmoniously keyed to exteriors.

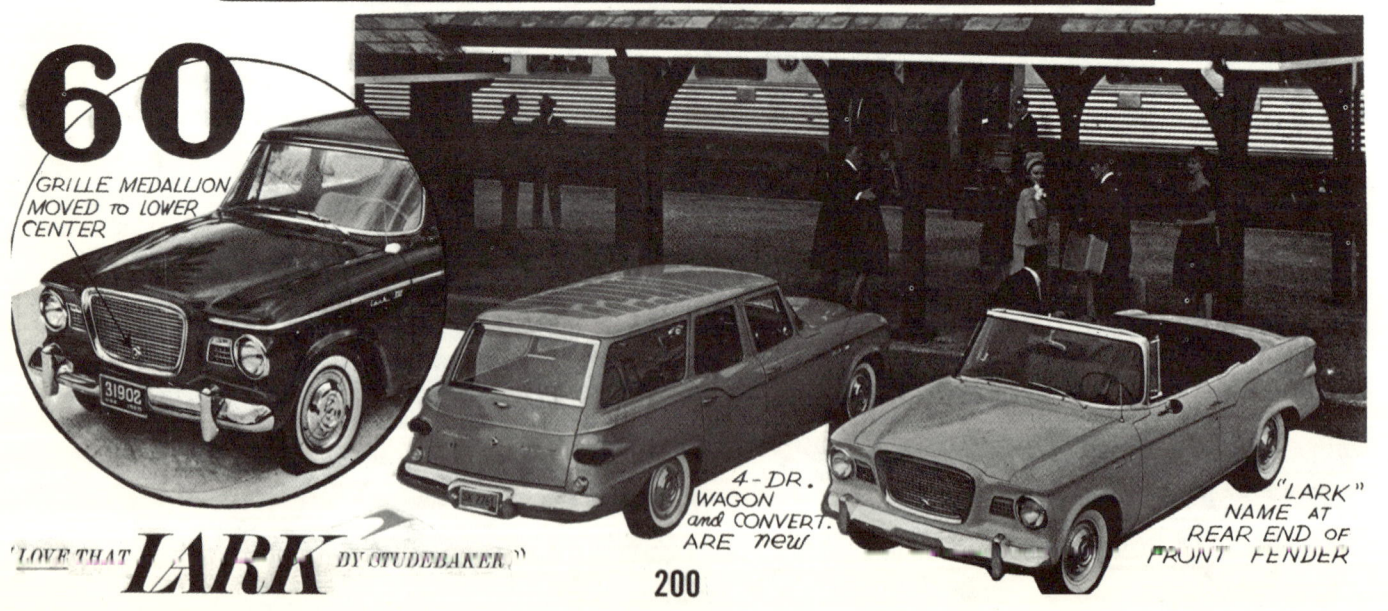

60

GRILLE MEDALLION MOVED TO LOWER CENTER

4-DR. WAGON and CONVERT. ARE new

"LARK" NAME AT REAR END OF FRONT FENDER

"LOVE THAT LARK BY STUDEBAKER"

200

LARK

61
- 4 HEADLIGHTS ON new 113" WB CRUISER
- 180 TO 225 HP
- 6 has 112 HP
- GRILLE EMBLEM MOVED; new PARK. LIGHTS; "LARK" NAME MOVED TO FORWARD END OF FR. FENDERS

"You have to drive The Lark to believe it!"

62
- 6 has 112 HP
- PACE CAR AT 1962 INDY 500 RACE
- DAYTONA CVT.
- new ROUND TAIL-LIGHTS
- "LARK" IN CAPITAL LETTERS
- DETAILS OF new GRILLE
- VIEWS OF DASH
- SUNROOF OPTIONAL ON new 225 HP DAYTONA

63
- SLIDING REAR ROOF SECTION ON new REGAL LARK WAGONAIRE
- new GRILLE AGAIN
- REGAL LARK
- LARK NAME USED ONLY 1959-1963
- SEE ALSO Studebaker

LINCOLN V-12 -ZEPHYR

LINCOLN CARS INTRODUCED LATE '20 (FOR 1921.) PRODUCT OF FORD MOTOR COMPANY (LINCOLN MOTOR CAR DIV.) SINCE 1921.

$1360.

V-12 ENGINES (THROUGH '48)

40

new 120 HP @ 3900 RPM

new 292.1 CID (THROUGH '41)

new 1-PIECE BACKLIGHT →

LINCOLN-ZEPHYR SERIES RUNS FROM 1936 THROUGH 1942 MODELS.

125" WB (SINCE '38)

$1400.

new SEALED BEAM HEADLIGHTS

LARGE, OLD-STYLE 150-HP "K" SERIES DISCONTINUED DURING 1940 SEASON, ALONG WITH ITS 414.1 CID ENGINE.

$2783.

CONTINENTAL COUPE

UNITIZED CONSTRUCTION OF BODY-AND-FRAME (IN CLOSED ZEPHYRS)

new CONTINENTAL
(FIRST FULL YEAR AVAIL. AS A REGULAR PRODUCTION MODEL)

CONTINENTAL has LOWER, BROADER BODY STYLING, AND SPARE TIRE IS MOUNTED OUTSIDE OF REAR DECK.

CONTINENTAL CABRIOLET

$2840.

202

7.00 x 16 TIRES
(SINCE '36)

COUPE

CLUB COUPE

LINCOLN
41

SEDAN

4.44 G.R.
(SINCE '38)

new CHROMED BORDER around GRILLE and new PARKING LTS. ATOP FRONT FENDERS

CONTINENTAL $2700.

$2675. CUSTOM (SEDAN OR LIMO.)
(LIMO.) SPECIAL 138" WB

new AUTOMATIC OVERDRIVE

BUTTON DOOR OPENERS now ON ALL

CONTINENTAL

new TALL HOOD MASCOT

new 30.5 CID
new 130 HP
@ 3800 RPM

42-45

new CHROME DECORATIONS AT EDGE OF REAR FENDERS (USED THROUGH '48)

new GRILLE

"The Finest Lincolns Ever Built"

new 7.00 x 15 TIRES

203

LINCOLN

← CONTINENTAL (PACE CAR AT 1946 INDY 500 RACE)

HEAVIER NAMEPLATE ON SIDES OF 1946 HOOD

46   66-H

PRICE RANGE:
$2178.
TO
$4205.

new HEAVIER GRILLE has BOTH HORIZ. and VERT. PCS.

125" WB AS BEFORE, BUT "ZEPHYR" NAME NO LONGER USED.

RAISED HEXAGON AT CENTER OF 1946 HUB CAPS

new LARGER BUMPERS

CONVENTIONAL DOOR HANDLES RETURN, ON STD. TYPES

"Nothing could be finer"

"Lincoln" NAME IN CHROME ON SIDES OF HOOD and ON new PLAINER HUBCAPS

FINAL LINCOLNS with V-12 ENGINES (1948)

7-H   8-H

47-48

CONTINENTAL

FINAL CONTINENTALS UNTIL 1956 MODEL

CONTINENTALS CONTINUE USE OF BUTTON DOOR OPENERS

$4380. ('48)
($200. INCR. FROM '47)

204

new 2-PC. WINDSHIELD (ON STANDARD LINCOLNS ONLY) (EL) $2527.

$3948.

new COSMOPOLITAN (EH)

49 (TOTALLY RESTYLED)

BACK SEAT AREA (COSMO.)

ALL with new V8 ENGINE (L-HEAD)

COSMOPOLITAN

121" WB LINC. "LIDO" CPE. IS new

new GRILLE IS LOWER

50

SOME MODELS PRICED ONLY $2 HIGHER THAN LAST YEAR'S

COSMO. "CAPRI" CPE. IS new

final COSMOPOLITAN 125" WB

new FULL-LENGTH CHROME MOULDING ALONG BODY SIDES OF COSMOPOLITAN MODELS (AND CONT'D. ON STD. LINCOLNS)

121" WB

51

new GRILLE

COSMO. SPORT SEDAN $3182.

LINCOLN SPORT SEDAN

205

LINCOLN

new 123" WB $3198.

H/T

CAPRI

COSMOPOLITAN

CVT. $3665.

52 (TOTALLY RESTYLED)

COSMO. IS NOW LOWER-PRICED SERIES, BELOW CAPRI.

"Lincoln" NAME IN SCRIPT LETTERING, ABOVE NEW GRILLE

$3226. COSMOPOLITAN

COSMOPOLITAN LETTERING DETAILS

53

CONV'T. DETAILS

CAPRI LETTERING DETAILS

CAPRI $3549.

NEW BLOCK "LINCOLN" LETTERING, ABOVE GRILLE WHICH NOW CONTAINS STYLIZED "V" AND SMALL EMBLEM

LINCOLN

new FENDER TRIM

54

new GRILLE

"LINCOLN" NAME NOW IN SCRIPT, and MOVED TO FRONT FENDER PANELS.

CONV'T.

CAPRI

CUSTOM is LOWER-PRICED SERIES, PRICED from $3563.

225 HP

new GRILLE with ALL HORIZONTAL PIECES

55

new 126" WB, new 285 HP

56

new PREMIERE

new PANORAMIC WINDSHIELD

CAPRI H/T

FRENCHED HEADLIGHTS, and new PARK./DIRECTIONAL LIGHTS IN GRILLE

new CHROME SIDE SPEAR

ALSO, A REVIVED **Continental**

(SEE NEXT PAGE)

LINCOLN

Continental Mark II

Continental Division · Ford Motor Company

$9538. ('56)
($157. MORE IN 1957.)

300 HP
126" WB

new CONTINENTAL STYLING DIFFERS FROM CAPRI, PREMIERE MODELS (THROUGH '60)

56-57

NON-CONTINENTAL 1957 TYPES: CAPRI PRICED FROM **$4649.**

COUPE (H/T)

PREMIERE CVT.

$5381.

LANDAU 4-DR. H/T

300 HP

57

208

CAPRI   new 131" WB (THROUGH '60)   PREMIERE

H/T $**4803**.

CONTINENTAL MARK III

Unmistakably... the finest in the fine car field

58 (TOTALLY RESTYLED)

new 375 HP

CONT'L. HAS new CRISS-CROSS GRILLE PATTERN

CONT'L. NO LONGER HAS "SPARE TIRE BULGE" IN REAR DECK

9.00 x 14 TIRES

$**6283**. (CVT.)

PREMIERE (CAPRI ALSO AVAIL.)

59 new GRILLE NOW ENCOMPASSES THE CANTED HEADLIGHTS

CUT TO 350 HP

CONTINENTAL MARK IV

$**7056**.

9.50 x 14 TIRES

LINCOLN

PREMIERE

2-DR. H/T

4-DR.

430 CID

HORSEPOWER CUT TO 315 @ 4100 RPM
(new CARBURETOR)
LEAF SPRINGS REPLACE COILS AT REAR

TYPICAL UPHOLSTERY (LEATHER and FABRICS)

new HOODED INSTRUMENTS

DASH and INSIDE DOOR HANDLE

60

CONTINENTAL MARK V

LANDAU 4-DR. H/T

2-DR. H/T

$5253. TO $10,230.
PRICE RANGE

FINAL YEAR FOR 2-DR. CONVERTIBLE

TOWN CAR

$9208.

LIMOUSINE

210

9.50 x 14 TIRES

LINCOLN CONTINENTAL

61
(TOTALLY RESTYLED)

new DASH

$6067.

REDUCTION OF WHEELBASE TO 123" (THROUGH '63) and CUT IN H.P. TO 300 @ 4100 RPM (THROUGH '62)

REAR

DECK LID OPENS WHEN TOP MOVES

$6713.

new Four-Door Convertible

ALL MODELS NOW KNOWN AS *Lincoln Continental*

new GRILLE and REAR END OF HARMONIZING DESIGN

62

211

LINCOLN (CONTINENTAL)

63

DETAIL OF CENTER-OPENING DOORS

4-DR. CONV'T. with TOP UP

new 320 HP (THROUGH '65)

LIMOUSINE

The luggage compartment is larger.

greater interior spaciousness

64
(SLIGHTLY ENLARGED)
new 126" WB (THROUGH '69)

3" LONGER THAN BEFORE

LIMO ROOFLINE

CONV. (CONTINUES THROUGH '67)

DASH

$6938.

65
new GRILLE with HORIZONTAL MOTIF

320 HP
430 CID

LINCOLN Continental
America's most distinguished motorcar.

212

Marlin BY RAMBLER — Newest of the Sensible Spectaculars
(ANNOUNCED 2-65)   **65**   (1965-1967)

116" WB
232 CID 6 (155 HP)
OR
287 CID V8 (198 HP)
OR
327 CID V8
270 HP @ 4700 RPM

POWER DISC BRAKES STANDARD

10,327 '65 MARLINS BLT.

WIRE WHEEL DETAIL

EASILY IDENTIFIED BY UNIQUE FASTBACK "KNIFE-EDGE" REAR STYLING

7.35 OR 7.75 × 14 TIRES

$3143. f.o.b. and up

Marlin GRILLE and SEATS (RECLINING)

Introducing excitement!
The swinging new man-size sports-fastback — MARLIN!

INTERIOR, THROUGH LONG SIDE WINDOW AREA

SEE ALSO: **RAMBLER**

213

MERCURY 8

MERCURY DIVISION OF FORD MOTOR COMPANY

STARTS with 1939 MODEL

116" WB (SINCE '39)

CVT. SEDAN ('40 ONLY)

SEDAN-COUPE

40

DASH is BLUE and SILVER

L-HEAD V8 ENGINE

OVERDRIVE AVAIL. $930.

new SEALED BEAM HEADLIGHTS

new VENT WINGS

CONTROLLED ALL-WEATHER VENTILATION

ENGINE

new 118" WB (THROUGH '51)

—THE AVIATION IDEA IN AN AUTOMOBILE

new GRILLE

41 RESTYLED

SPARE TIRE and WHEEL STOWED VERTICALLY AGAINST WALL

new 1-PC. BACKLIGHT

CONT'D. NEXT PAGE

214

MERCURY

41 (CONT'D.)

MORE ROOM — Wherever extra size contributes to comfort, Mercury is big. More head, leg and seat room enables passengers to relax and rest in perfect comfort as they ride.

$920.

SMART NEW STATION WAGON is a brand-new Mercury body type this year. Front end and driver's compartment follow the sedan styling. Body is of selected maple and birch. Choice of tan, blue or red hand-buffed leather upholstery. Large luggage capacity. White sidewall tires extra.

THE BIG CAR THAT STANDS ALONE IN ECONOMY

42-45

More Power Per Pound

new 6.50 x 15 TIRES

new 2-TIER GRILLE

NEW *Liquamatic Drive* (OPT.)

DOUBLE CHROME BANDS on FENDERS

46

$2078.

WOODEN BODY PANELS ON new SPORTSMAN

new GRILLE

new GRILLE

new INTERIORS

$1412.

CONT'D NEXT PAGE

215

MERCURY 46 (CONT'D.)

$1390. "COUPE-SEDAN"

"STEP OUT WITH MERCURY"

ALL-STEEL CONVERTIBLE $1604.

INTERIORS ('47)

47-48

WAGON $1676.

BORDER OF GRILLE IS NOW CHROME-PLATED

More OF EVERYTHING YOU WANT

WITH *Mercury*

216

MERCURY

new 2-DR. WAGON

49 TOTALLY RESTYLED
110 HP

Make your next car *Mercury*
FROM $1997.

new EMBLEMS AT EITHER END

"Better than ever"

50 PACE CAR AT 1950 INDY 500 RACE

LARGE PARK. LIGHTS AT ENDS OF GRILLE

Nothing like it on the Road!

new GRILLE and new EMBLEMS

51 new OPTIONAL **MERC-O-MATIC** AUTO. TRANS. 217   LARGER BACKLIGHT

new VERT. TAIL-LIGHTS

for "the buy of your life!"

MERCURY Merc-O-Matic Drive...or B-W Overdrive

CUSTOM

MONTEREY hardtop H/T

NEW 125 H.P. HIGH-COMPRESSION V-8

new DASH

52 (TOTALLY RESTYLED)

FROM $1987.

new HOOD SCOOP

new BUMPER-GRILLE

new SHORTER 115" WB

new DECK-LID MEDALLION

POWER STEERING

DASH

POWER BRAKES

new HORIZ. REAR FENDER TRIM

3 new POWER OPTION CHOICES

53

new GRILLE, 118" WB

4-WAY POWER SEAT

218

(CONT'D.)

MERCURY

$2057.

CUSTOM
(LOWER-PRICED THAN Monterey SER.)

53 (CONT'D.)

GET THE FACTS — AND YOU'LL GO FOR THE NEW 1953 **MERCURY**

CUSTOM SEDANS

MONTEREY

new 161-horsepower engine

DASH

$2581.

"SUN VALLEY" (new)

THE CAR THAT MAKES ANY DRIVING EASY

54

new GRILLE

CUSTOM

new REAR STYLING

MONTEREY

new PANORAMIC WINDSHIELD

new 188 HP

new SIDE TRIM

55 FROM $2218.

new GRILLE and HOODED HEADLIGHTS

new 119" WB

new MONTCLAIR

SUN VALLEY

219

MERCURY

For 1956 — the big move is to THE BIG MERCURY

56

- MEDALIST (new)
- MONTEREY
- CUSTOM
- VOYAGER (in Montclair SERIES)
- "PHAETON" 4-DR. HARDTOP — $2507.
- REAR 3/4 DETAIL
- MONTCLAIR
- new 210 HP
- new GRILLE (CLOSE-UP)
- interior

220

MERCURY BIG M for '57

QUADRI-BEAM HEADLAMPS (LATER MODELS)
- HIGH BEAM
- LOW or HIGH BEAM

(EARLY, MONTCLAIR)

MONTEREY

PACE CAR AT 1957 INDY 500 RACE

57 with DREAM-CAR DESIGN (LATER)

(TOTALLY RESTYLED) new 122" WB 255 HP

FRONT ROOF VENTS ON TURNPIKE CR. (290 HP)

CONVENTIONAL STATION WAGON | NEW BIG M STATION WAGON

MERCURY ELIMINATES THE LIFT GATE, LOWERS THE TAIL GATE

new **TURNPIKE CRUISER**

THERE'S ONLY ONE SIDE PILLAR IN THE NEW MERCURY COMMUTER

VOYAGER — 2 and 4-DR. WAGONS

THE OPEN-AIR FEELING OF A HARDTOP

ONLY 2 HEADLIGHTS ON EARLY MODELS

COLONY PARK $3677.

6 wagons

BIG new WEDGE TAIL-LIGHTS

CENTER OF BACKLIGHT OPENS, ON TURNPIKE CR.

5-7. NEW MONITOR CONTROL PANEL, TACHOMETER, AVERAGE SPEED COMPUTER

221

MERCURY

PRICED FROM $2547.

THE ALL-NEW PARK LANE

58 — WHEEL COVER

122" WB (126" on Park Lane)

20th ANNIVERSARY '59 MERCURY

"BUILT TO LEAD — BUILT TO LAST"

59

ENGINE

new GRILLE VARIES IN APPEARANCE, DEPENDING ON ANGLE FROM WHICH IT IS VIEWED (SEE ALSO NEXT PG.)

new ENLARGED WINDSHIELD AREA

222

(CONT'D.)

MERCURY

MONTEREY SEDAN

MONTCLAIR

59 (CONT'D.)

FANCIER REAR STYLING ON MONTCLAIR

PARK LANE 4-DR. H/T CRUISER (ABOVE) has SPECIAL REAR SIDE TRIM

VOYAGER

COMMUTER

WHEEL COVER

126" WB (128" on Park Lane)

COLONY PARK $3932. (6-PASS.)

$3330. (9-PASS.)

SLIP THE THIRD SEAT UNDER THE FLOOR

WAGON DETAILS

COMMUTER

223

MERCURY

FROM $2631. 2-DR. H/T (MONTEREY)

MONTCLAIR

MONTEREY

(RESTYLED) **60** 4-DR H/T (MONTEREY)

9-PASS. COMMUTER $3240.

9-PASS. COLONY PARK $3950.

$3858.

PARK LANE 4-DR. H/T

$4018.

PARK LANE CVT. CHROME PCS. IDENTIFY MODEL SERIES

126" WB ON ALL MERCURYS (1960 ONLY)

MERCURY

METEOR 600
new series
V8 or new 6

METEOR 800

the better low-price cars

61

MODEL NAME at FRONT END of DOOR
Meteor 800

MONTEREY

MONTEREY

COMMUTER

COLONY PARK

METEOR 62

S-33 DASH

METEOR

MONTEREY CUSTOM

new GRILLES

S-33 WHEEL COVER

MONTEREY

new TAIL-LIGHTS AT TOP OF FENDERS

MERCURY

METEOR

FINAL METEOR. 6-CYL. MERC. ENG. ONLY IN COMET AFTER '63.

METEOR S-33

MONTEREY

H/T

4-DR H/T

new OPENING "BREEZEWAY" BACKLIGHT

CONSOLE (S-55)

63

S-55 and INTERIOR

MONTRY. CUSTOM MARAUDER ('63½)

METEOR CUSTOM

COUNTRY CRUISER

COLONY PARK and INTERIOR

226

MERCURY

V8s ONLY

No finer car in the medium-price field

Commuter station wagon

COLONY PARK

2-DR. H/T

MONTEREY
FROM $3202.
120" WB (ALL MOD.)

250 HP V8

64

4-DR. MARAUDER H/T
$3567.

MONTCLAIR

2-DR. H/T (BREEZEWAY ROOFLINE)

CLOSE-UP OF DOOR — (PARK LANE) SHOWN ABOVE

$3799.
4-DR. MARAUDER H/T

PARK LANE (300 HP)
INTERIOR →

2-DR. H/T (BREEZEWAY ROOFLINE)

-227-

DASH

MERCURY

NOW IN THE LINCOLN CONTINENTAL TRADITION

TOTALLY RESTYLED '65

AMERICAN MOTORS IMPORTED
Metropolitan (1954-1961)

"HOOD SCOOP"

ASSEMBLED IN ENGLAND BY AUSTIN, FOR U.S. MARKET

4 CYL., O.H.V. AUSTIN ENGINE

$1445. TO $1749.
(DURING '54 TO '61)

54-55
42 HP

TYPE CONT. TO EARLY 1956

OUTSIDE TRUNK DOOR ADDED DURING 1959 MODEL YEAR

56-61
new GRILLE and SIDE TRIM

CONVERTIBLE

52 HP

COUPE

AT YOUR **RAMBLER-METROPOLITAN** *DEALER*

228

MUSTANG

ROY C. McCARTHY,
MUSTANG ENGINEERING CO.,
SEATTLE AND RENTON, WASH.

(1947-1949)

49

4-CYL. HERCULES ENGINE
59 H.P.   65 M.P.H.
NO DEALERSHIPS; FACTORY ORDERS ONLY

ALUMINUM BODY
102" W.B.
5.50 x 15" TIRES

MUSTANG Ford

(STARTS APRIL, 1964)

65

6 OR V8
(170 CID) (260 CID)

STD. TYPE w/o GRILLE LIGHTS →

standard-equipment
(bucket seats, full carpeting, vinyl interior, floor-mounted transmission)

CVT. IS PACE CAR AT 1964 INDY 500 RACE.

WHEEL COVER

Surprisingly spacious trunk

REAR

STANDARD DASH (ABOVE)

$2368* f.o.b. Detroit
AND UP

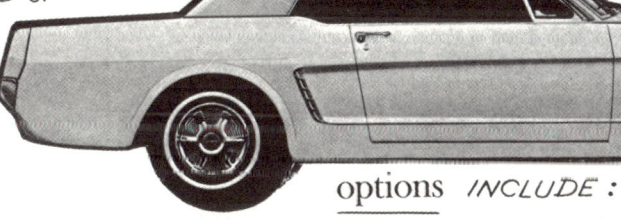

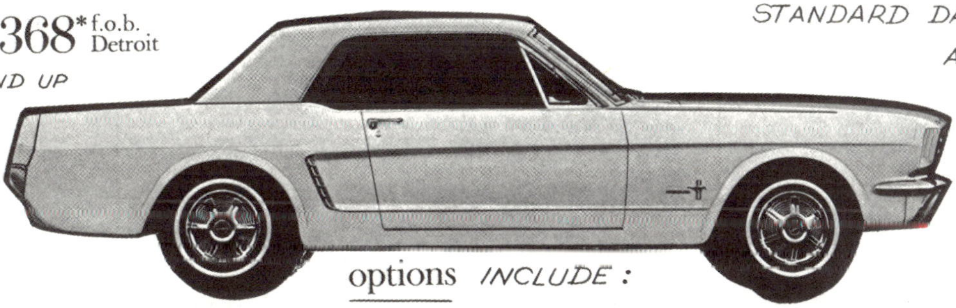

ALL CIRCULAR GAUGES ON DE LUXE DASH (BELOW)

options INCLUDE:
a 289 cu. in. V-8. Four-on-the-floor. Tachometer and clock combo. Special handling package. Front disc brakes —

New luxury instrument panel

STANDARD SIDE EMBLEM

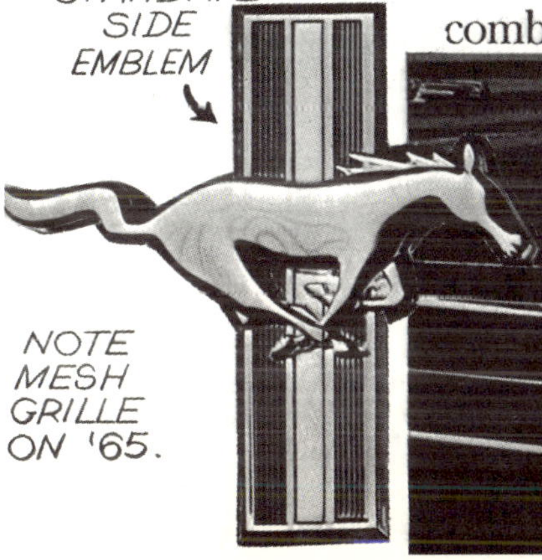

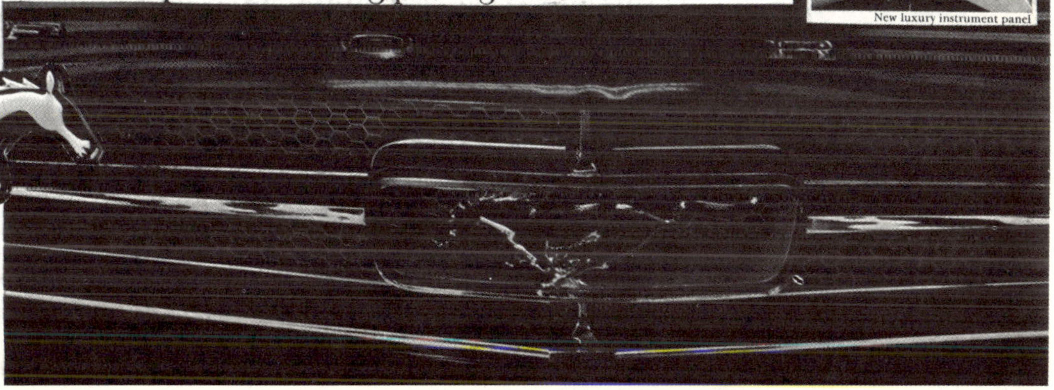

NOTE MESH GRILLE ON '65.

MUSTANG

Unique Ford GT stripe — badge of America's greatest total performance cars!

New integral arm rests — courtesy lights

INTERIOR VIEWS (ABOVE)

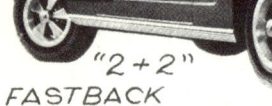

"2+2" FASTBACK

NOTCHBACK HARDTOP

Mustang GT

CONVERTIBLE

65 (CONT'D.)

EXTRA (FOG) LIGHTS IN GT GRILLE

IDENTIFYING RACING STRIPES ON GT →

MUSTANG

(VINYL-COVERED ROOF AVAIL.)

NASH MOTORS—Division of Nash-Kelvinator Corporation, Detroit

Again.. it's that new NASH

6 CYL. OR STRAIGHT-8

SEDAN

(1917 — 1957)

(ALSO BLT. LAFAYETTE LOWER-PRICED MODELS, 1934-1940)

$795. and up

1940 IS FINAL YEAR FOR 2-PIECE BACKLIGHT IN CLOSED NASH CARS

(THE FINAL) LAFAYETTE 6

117" WB
4.1 GR

COACH
4013

40

OVERDRIVE AVAIL.

AMBASSADOR 6 AVAIL. (121" WB)

"BUSTLE-BACK" SEDAN, SHOWING BACK SEAT BED AVAILABLE →

AMBASSADOR 8
125" WB

COUPE 4085

4081
CABRIOLET

"Weather Eye"
HEATER-COOLER AVAIL. (SINCE '38)

63,617 BLT. 1940

DASH

"SPECIAL" ROADSTER

231

NASH 600 80, 408 BLT. 1941

Now—coil springs on rear wheels, too!

4149
$745 BUYS

"Go NASH AND SAVE MONEY EVERY MILE"

41

AS BEFORE, FIRST 2 DIGITS IN MODEL NO. SIGNIFY THE YEAR (SINCE '35)

AMBASSADOR

Nash IN RED LETTERING ON BUMPER and HUBCAPS

4183 (8)

CLUB COUPE KNOWN AS "BROUGHAM"

REAR

SINCE '41 "600s," UNITIZED BODY-AND FRAME CONSTRUCTION

31,700 BLT.

4240

42-45

FINAL STRAIGHT 8 NASH MODELS

232

NASH

NOW 6-CYL. ONLY (THROUGH '54)

46

600 DLX. — 112" WB L-HEAD ENG. — 4640

121" WB 112 HP OHV — 4663

AMBASSADOR
PROD. 6148 (LATER '45)
98,769 (DURING '46)

new MEDALLION and PK. LITES

new GRILLE

MODEL 4664 AMB. SUBURBAN SEDAN with WOODEN PANELING

47

AMBASS. SEDAN IS PACE CAR AT 1947 INDY 500 RACE

4740 (600)
4760 (AMB.)

EL SEGUNDO, CALIF. and TORONTO, ONT. BRANCH PLANTS PURCHASED THE PRECEDING YR. MEXICO CITY PLANT OPENS 6-18-47.

4748 (fastback)
4740 (bustle-back)

"You'll be Ahead with Nash"

new CHROMED EXTENSIONS AT EITHER SIDE OF UPPER GRILLE PORTION

PROD.: 113,315

48

600 — 4842 — COUPE

EXCEPT ON "600," new HIGHER BELT LINE CHROME FOR 1948

SUPER "FASTBACK" SEDAN — 4868

new CVT. (1,000 BLT.) AMBASSADOR — 4871

"BUSTLE BACK" SEDAN — 4840

4863 or 4843

DASH (MORE DETAILS NEXT PAGE)

MORE '48 DETAILS ON NEXT PAGE

233

NASH

48 (CONT'D.)
118,621 BLT.

FULL VIEW OF INTERIOR

You'll be Ahead with Nash

Great Cars Since 1902

"SUPER" and "CUSTOM" are new

AMB. SUPER (MODEL NAME ON SIDE OF HOOD.)

4860

600 82 HP
4949

has "600" IN CHROME, ON FRONT FENDER PANEL.

EL SEGUNDO, CALIF. PLANT OPENS 10-48

49
TOTALLY RESTYLED new *Airflyte* MODELS (NO CVTS.)

PHANTOM VIEW

142,592 BLT.

ONE SINGLE WELDED UNIT!

with Girder-built Unitized Body and Frame... Airliner-styled interiors... Cockpit Control... Uniscope... Matched Coil Springs on all Four Wheels... Twin Beds... Uniflo-Jet Carb

AMBASSADOR 112 HP

234

NASH WITH *HYDRA-MATIC DRIVE*

BACKLIGHTS ENLARGED

191,865 BLT.

The Ambassador Custom 115 HP

The Statesman 85 HP
(REPLACES 600)

50

new SLIDING GLOVE DRAWER
THICKER BUMPER GUARDS

...NEW SUPER-POWER ENGINES!

new **Rambler** also avail. AT NASH DEALERS

Airflytes for 1951

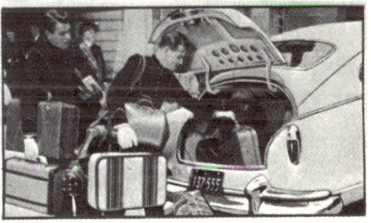

5148
STATESMAN

5159

51

New sky-flow fenders

TRUNK DETAILS

new BUMPERS
new GRILLE with VERTICAL PCS.

5169
AMBASSADOR SUPER

5168

RECLINING SEATS
(with BODY CENTERPOST NOT SHOWN, IN ORDER THAT SEAT DETAIL CAN BE SEEN.)

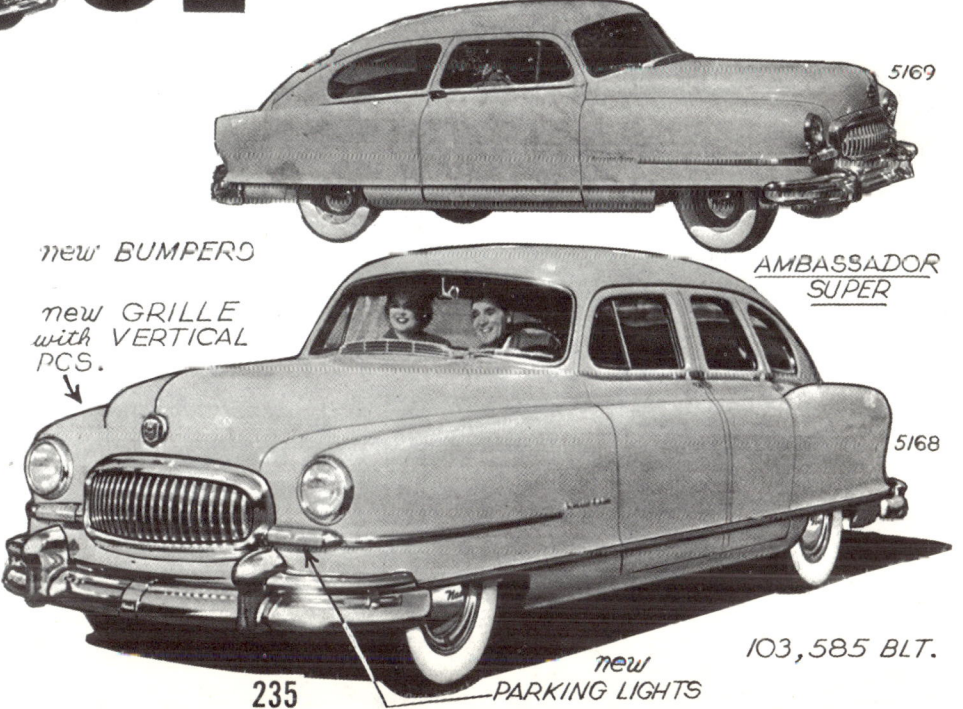

235

new PARKING LIGHTS

103,585 BLT.

NASH
(TOTALLY RESTYLED FOR 1952)

Golden Airflytes
50TH ANNIVERSARY (OF RAMBLERS)

Pinin Farina, STYLIST

new 88 HP

('52)
5255

new 114¼" WB
STATESMAN CUSTOM

AMBASSADOR CUSTOM ← 120 HP

5275
new 121¼" WB

52-53
152,141 BLT.*   153,753 BLT.*   *= INCL. RMB.

5355
('53) 100 HP

'53 WITH NEW STRIPS OF CHROME ON VENT

DASH ('53)

('53) AMBASSADOR COUNTRY CLUB
5377

Ambassador Country Club

110 HP STATESMAN SUPER

67,192 BLT.

54

130 HP AMBASSADOR SUPER
5465

5446
new BORDERS AROUND MODIFIED GRILLE

5475

ST. OR AM. CUST. MODELS HAVE REAR-MOUNTED "CONTINENTAL" SPARE TIRE.

AMERICAN MOTORS CORP. FORMED BY MAY 1, 1954 NASH–HUDSON MERGER.

AMBASSADOR CUSTOM

236

'55 NASH

STATESMAN SUPER 5545-1

CNTRY. CLUB 5547-2

5585-1

(RESTYLED) Scena-Ramic WINDSH.

AMBASSADOR SUPER

new "INBOARD" HEADLIGHTS

5585-2   57,619 BLT.

AMB. CUSTOM
208-HP V8
PACKARD ENG. OPTIONAL

STATESMAN SUPER   5645-1   **Ambassador Special**

130 HP

56

5665-1 (6)

AMBASSADOR SUPER 6

AMBASSADOR CUSTOM V8

5655-2

Torque-Flo V-8

5657-1

THE NEW *Ambassador Special*
WITH NEW A.M.C.-BUILT V8
190 HP
250 CID   (INTRO. 4-56)

237

NASH

AMBASSADOR COUNTRY CLUB

PHOTOGRAPHED IN DISNEYLAND

56 (CONT'D.)

DELUXE, SUPER, or CUSTOM 6 REPLACE STATESMAN 6 MODELS

AMBASSADOR SUPER

V-8

5785-1

new GRILLE and SIDE TRIM

255 HP

57

THE FINAL NASH

5787-2

AMBASSADOR CUSTOM

121½" WB

- New wider front tread for surer footing
- New sharper, easier turning
- Airliner Reclining Seats
- All-Season Air Conditioning
- Choice of Hydramatic, Overdrive or Standard
- Twin Travel Beds

5785-2

← new STACKED HEADLIGHTS

SUPERSEDED BY RAMBLER

JOIN THE SWING TO THE TRAVEL KING

'57 *Nash* World's Finest Travel Car

238

OLDS F-85
BY OLDSMOBILE
(COMPACT)

(STARTS 1961)

155 STD. HP

ENTIRE REAR DOOR RAISES, ON WAGON

61

112" WB
6.50 x 13 TIRES
3.36 GEAR RATIO

F-85 Cutlass

Above: F-85 Cutlass Sports Coupe. Also available: new F-85 Club Coupe...

new ROCKETTE 185 Engine
(ALUMINUM BLOCK)
185 HP V8
10.25 COMPR.
4 BBL. CARB.

F-85 SEDAN
$2713.

"...it's every inch an OLDSMOBILE"

OLDS F-85 →

F-85 COUPE

CUTLASS COUPE

CUTLASS

$ **2949.**
(SAME PRICE AS LAST YEAR)

62

F-85 COUPE

CUTLASS H/T

CVT.

WAGON

JETFIRE H/T
(note HEAVIER SIDE TRIM)

new SHAPE OF TAIL-LIGHT

TO 195 HP with ALUMINUM V8

DELUXE SEDAN

63

new GRILLE with "OLDSMOBILE" NAME ACROSS CENTER STRIP

OLDS F-85 →

There's 'Something Extra' about owning an OLDSMOBILE!

WAGON (DLX.) OLDS F-85 CUTLASS new 230 HP F-85 V-6 SPORTS COUPE

VISTA-CRS.

WHERE THE ACTION IS!

WIRE WH. COVERS AVAIL.

new VISTA-CRUISER WAGON has ROOF WINDOWS

64 V8 or V6

new ECON-O-WAY V-6

SEDAN PROFILE

JETAWAY DRIVE

an all-new transmission

JETFIRE ROCKET V-8

Vista-Cruiser

CUTLASS

65

4-4-2 has 400 CID V8

442

CUTLASS

VISTA-CRUISER has FOLDING, FORWARD-FACING 3RD SEAT
Roomy cargo area—holds over 100 cubic feet!

1965 The Rocket Action Car!

241

OLDSMOBILE (SINCE 1897)

Product of GENERAL MOTORS

OLDS PRICES START AT **$807** up, FOR "60" BUSINESS COUPE (PAINTED HORIZ. PCS. IN GRILLE OF "60")

6 OR 8-CYL. L-HEAD ENGINES

40

new SEALED-BEAM HEADLAMPS

116" WB 6.00 x 16

"*Bigger* and *Better* in Everything!"

WITH *Hydra-Matic Drive* AUTOMATIC TRANSMISSION (OPT.)

NO GEARS TO SHIFT!

124" WB

CUSTOM 8 CRUISER (90)

7.00 x 16

70

120" WB

229.7 CID 6 (SINCE '37) 95 HP @ 3400 RPM
OR
257.1 CID 8 (SINCE '37) 110 HP @ 3600 RPM

"BEST LOOKING CAR ON THE ROAD!"

THE CAR *Ahead!*

STYLED TO LEAD — BUILT TO LAST

new 238.1 CID 6 (100 HP @ 3400)

41

new 119" or 125" WB

SPECIAL 60

new "SPECIAL 60" TOWN SEDAN (66 SER.)

6.00 x 16

$852., and up, f.o.b.

242 (CONT'D.)

41 (CONT'D.) HYDRA-MATIC

ABOVE PLATE IDENTIFIES CARS with AUTO. TRANS.

STRAIGHT-8 ENGINE SPECS. AS IN '40.

PROVED AND IMPROVED FOR "42":
HYDRA-MATIC DRIVE*
THE GENERAL MOTORS CONTRIBUTION TO SIMPLER, SAFER, MORE EFFICIENT DRIVING!

NO GEARS TO SHIFT! NO CLUTCH TO PRESS!

119", 125", OR 127" WB

"B-44" SERIES 42

NEW 4U-4-42

(CONT'D.)

243

OLDSMOBILE

SPECIAL 66

$960., f.o.b.

42 (CONT'D.)

ENGINE SPECS. AS BEFORE

INTERIOR

OLDSMOBILE IS TURNING OUT CANNON FOR FIGHTING PLANES — SHELL FOR THE ARTILLERY

DYNAMIC CRUISER

"YOU CAN ALWAYS COUNT ON OLDSMOBILE —

— IT'S QUALITY-BUILT TO LAST!"

CHROME TRIM ELIMINATED

WARTIME "BLACKOUT" MODEL →

42½ - 45

OLDSMOBILE

A NEW AND FINER **HYDRA-MATIC DRIVE** (GM General Motors)

INTERIOR

76

66 CLUB SEDAN 119" WB

98 125" WB

46
$1290. and up, f.o.b. (66 CL.CPE.) ($95. MORE IN '47)

ENGINE SPECS. (6 and 8) AS SINCE '41

66 STATION WAGON $2305. f.o.b.

68

98 CUSTOM CRUISER CVT. $2160., f.o.b.

119", 125" OR 127" WB (THROUGH '48)

LONGER RED SECTION AROUND "OLDSMOBILE" NAME IN FRONT FENDER CHROME STRIP

47

CENTER SECTION OF BUMPER NO LONGER GROOVED AT TOP

It's *Smart* to own an Olds

245

OLDSMOBILE

$1385. and up, f.o.b. (66 CL. CPE. or 2-DR.)

119" or 125" WB on OLD-STYLED 6 and 8

76 (6-CYL.)

48

RETAINS 1947-STYLE BODY, BUT has "OLDSMOBILE" NAME and new CIRCLE EMBLEM ABOVE GRILLE, and NEW-STYLE CHROME SIDE TRIM.

new FUTURAMIC

"98" MODELS TOTALLY RESTYLED

127" WB

98 (OLDSMOBILE'S FINAL CARS with STRAIGHT-8 ENGINE)

"FUTURAMIC" NAME BEGINS WITH THE 8-CYL. RESTYLED 1948 OLDSMOBILES, AND IS USED FOR A FEW YEARS AFTERWARDS.

$1740., f.o.b. 2-DR. CLUB SEDAN

$2160., f.o.b.

98 CONVERTIBLE has new HYDRAULICALLY OPERATED POWER SIDE WINDOWS and AUTOMATIC FRONT SEAT ADJUSTER

FUTURAMIC

246

OLDSMOBILE

$1732., and up, f.o.b. (76 CL. CP.)

New NEW *ROCKET* ENGINE! (O.H.V V8)

135 HP (TO '52)

76

105 HP
119½" WB
6

98 (125" WB)

49

new AIR SCOOPS BELOW HEADLIGHTS

new "HOLIDAY" H/T $2973. f.o.b.

You've got to drive it to believe it!

"88" DESIGNATION USUALLY ON REAR FENDER

UNLIKE "98," THE NEW '49½ "88" has CURVED LOWER EDGES OF WINDSHIELD

NEW **"88"** (49½ INTRO. AFTER SEASON UNDER WAY)

LOWEST-PRICED CAR WITH "ROCKET" ENGINE

$2375., f.o.b. 88 DLX. SEDAN

"The New Thrill"

THIS IDENTIFIES V8 MODELS

"88" 119½" WB

CVT. IS PACE CAR AT 1949 INDY 500 RACE

247

OLDSMOBILE ROCKETS AHEAD

FINAL 6-CYL. "76" has NO CHROME STRIP on FRONT FENDER

$1761., and up, f.o.b. (76 2-DR.)

OLDSMOBILE "88"

50

88

88 CVT. **$2294.,** f.o.b.

98

8.20 × 15 TIRES ON 98 CVT.

Make a Date with a "Rocket 8"!

NEW! SUPER "88"

51

135 HP

V8s ONLY (119½" WB ON 88 ONLY)

7.60 × 15 TIRES (88, SU-88)

$1970., and up, f.o.b. (88 2-DR.)

248 (CONT'D.)

CVT. $**2673**., f.o.b.

SUPER "88" 120" WB

2 DR.
$**2265**., f.o.b.

51
(CONT'D.)

"ROCKET" **98** 122" WB

New Room Inside!

DLX. HOLIDAY H/T
$**2882**., f.o.b.

$**2610**., f.o.b.

249

88

$2262., f.o.b. 2-DR. 120" WB

$2462., f.o.b. SU-88 SEDAN

The "Rocket" Oldsmobile's New Power Steering* makes driving so easy you can...

Park with just 1 finger!

SU-88 H/T

HORIZ. GROOVES ON SU-88 FENDER PAD; VERTICAL GROOVES ON 98.

SUPER 88

new VERTICAL "TOOTH" AT CENTER OF GRILLE

52

new SIDE TRIM (SEE DETAILS)

98 TAIL-LIGHT

Ninety-Eight SEDAN $2786., f.o.b.

124" WB 160 HP
new "SUPER" RANGE in Hydra-Matic

$3229., f.o.b. CVT.

Ninety Eight H/T

OLDSMOBILE

REAR QUARTER DETAILS (SEDAN) 98

new SIDE TRIM DESIGN IDENTIFIES '52

250

OLDSMOBILE

88 2-DR.

88 has 150 HP @ 3600 RPM

$2262., f.o.b.

FINAL YR. FOR 303 CID V8s

53

H/T

DETAILS OF SUPER 88 HOLIDAY H/T

DETAILS OF THE 1953 ENGINE

SUPER 88

SEDAN

SU-88, 98 have 165 HP @ 3600 RPM

CVT. 3229., f.o.b.

Ninety-Eight

AIR COND. AVAIL.

Holiday H/T

$3022., f.o.b.

POWER BRAKES and POWER STEERING ORDERED on MOST UNITS.

251

OLDSMOBILE

$2237., and up, f.o.b.

88

new PANORAMIC WINDSHIELDS ON ALL

SUPER 88

HOLIDAY COUPÉ

170 HP @ 4000 (88)
185 HP @ 4000 (SU-88, 98)

ALL with new 324 CID V8s. (THROUGH '56)

54 (RESTYLED)

98

122" WB (88, SU-88)
126" WB (98)

98 STARFIRE CVT.

Ninety-Eight

REAR DETAILS (98)

$3248., f.o.b.

INTERIOR OF NEW *"Starfire"* 185 HP

LARGE, BOXY DECK AREA

1954

252

OLDSMOBILE 55

$2362., f.o.b.
SEDAN

88 185 HP INT.

OLDSMOBILE'S ENTIRELY NEW

SUPER 88

Holiday Sedan — A HARDTOP...WITH 4 DOORS

IT'S A HOLIDAY... with Sedan convenience!
IT'S A SEDAN... with Holiday smartness!

Ninety Eight

NEW! ALL-AROUND new 202 HP ENG. (SU-88, 98)

56 88

FINAL YR. FOR 324 CID V8 (230 OR 240 HP @ 4400 RPM)

INTERIOR

(CONT'D ON NEXT PAGE)

"Holiday" new BISECTED GRILLE

88 2-DR.
$2338., and up, f.o.b.

253

OLDSMOBILE
SUPER 88

$2484., f.o.b.
SU-88 2-DR.

98 4-DR. H/T DLX. HOLIDAY SEDAN

56 (CONT'D.)

$3456., f.o.b.

GOLDEN ROCKET

GOLDEN ROCKET 88

f.o.b. PRICES START AT **$2691.** (88 2-DR.)

277 HP @ 4400 RPM WITH *new* 371 CID V8 (371 CID AVAIL. THROUGH '60)

57 (RESTYLED)

new TAIL-LIGHTS and SIDE TRIM

8.50 x 14 TIRES (THROUGH '58)

new SUPER 88 FIESTA

SUPER 88

$3499., f.o.b.

new GRILLE

122" WB (126" on 98)

$3887., f.o.b.

← note 3-PC. BACKLIGHT on H/T (new)

new **Startfire 98** H/T

254

OLDSMOBILE 88

FIESTA 88

DYNAMIC 88
SUPER 88
NINETY-EIGHT
16 models to choose from!

(TOTALLY RESTYLED)

122½" OR 126½" WB

SUPER 88

265, 305 OR 312 HP

58

BADGE ON SU-88 and 98

98 for '58

THE "CHROME KING" OF ALL CARS!

New Rocket Engine is more powerful, gives greater performance than ever before. In addition, carburetion advances provide you with an opportunity for improved fuel savings, as much as 20%!

"OLDSmobility"

$2772., and up, f.o.b.

DASH DETAILS

New Trans-Portable® — a transistor radio that serves as your regular car radio, operating on car's built-in circuit, can also be unlocked and carried from car as a compact, lightweight portable.

New Safety-Vee Steering Wheel, with modern two-spoke, safety recessed design, allows unobstructed view of vital instrument panel gauges. New twin horn buttons are located within easy reach.

Dual-Range Power Heater® gives the exact amount of heat or ventilation exactly where you want it . . . when you want it. You merely touch a button . . . power does all the work for you!

*Optional at extra cost.

4 HEADLTS. ABOVE new GRILLE

new "LINEAR" LOOK
LTS. SEPERATED within new GRILLE

371 CID (270 HP @ 4600)
OR
new 394 CID
(315 HP @ 4600)

59

(TOTALLY RESTYLED AGAIN)

$2837., and up, f.o.b.

(CONT'D.)

255

OLDSMOBILE

59 (CONT'D.)

DYN. 88 HOLIDAY SCENICOUPE H/T

4-DR.
DYNAMIC 88
2-DR.
← DY-88 HAS NO ROCKER PANEL CHROME (LENGTH EXAGGERATED)

FIESTA

SUPER 88

4-DR. H/T HOLIDAY SPORTSEDANS

new 9.00 × 14 TIRES ON SU-88, 98

98

ninety-eight 4-door sedan

98 CVT. ↑
$4366.
f.o.b.

98 HOLIDAY SCENICOUPE H/T

DASH

$2900., f.o.b.
88 CELEBRITY 4-DR. SEDAN
DYNAMIC 88
FIESTA WAGON
SUPER 88

OLDSMOBILE 60
PACE CAR AT 1960 INDY 500 RACE

98

with *Roto-Matic Power Steering*

240 OR 315 HP @ 4600 RPM
(FINAL YR. FOR SMALLER (371) V8)

GO OLDS '60!

DASH

SU-88 FIESTA WAGON

OLDSMOBILE

power features and accessories for your driving pleasure

WINDOW SWITCHES

RADIO

Other Oldsmobile Options include such convenience features as: Guide-Matic Power Headlight Control, Safety Sentinel, Swivel Dome and Reading Lamp, Deck Lid Power Lock Release, Electric Ventipanes, De Luxe Wheel Discs, Trim Rings and Air Conditioning.

POWER HEATER

MANUAL HEATER

Starglo Moroccean interiors—optional at no extra cost in both Dynamic 88 Holiday Sedans and Holiday Coupes. And this long-wearing, easy-to-clean all-vinyl trim is as handsome as it is durable.

THIS REAR-END STYLING IN 1961 ONLY

$3359., f.o.b.

DYNAMIC 88   123" WB   250 HP

POWER ANTENNA

61 (TOTALLY RESTYLED)

DYNAMIC 88 FIESTA (AVAILABLE IN 2 AND 3-SEAT MODELS)

Super 88

OLDSMOBILE 123" WB

Skyrocket PERFORMANCE!

new "Skyrocket" ENGINE (394 CID V8) 325 HP @ 4600 RPM 10 TO 1 COMPRESSION (USED IN SU-88, 98; OPTIONAL IN DY-88)

DISTINGUISHED...
DISTINCTIVE...
DECIDEDLY NEW!

DASH

Foam-padded pattern cloth, handsomely accented with lustrous *lemeltone* 88, adds brilliant new sparkle to this super 88 Holiday Sedan. Five harmonizing color choices are available.

"OLDSMOBILE" NAME BELOW new GRILLE (ON 88s)

258

(98 MODELS ON NEXT PAGE)

OLDSMOBILE

61 (CONT'D.)

INTERIOR

V8

CLASSIC 98 SPORT SEDAN

STARFIRE (new)

CLASSIC 98
126" WB

CLASSIC 98 TOWN SEDAN

98

WHEEL COVER (98)

REAR QUARTER DETAIL

CLASSIC 98 HOLIDAY SEDAN

(LENGTH EXAGGERATED)

H/T

DYNAMIC 88

4-DR. H/T

WAGON has UNIQUE REAR FENDER DESIGN

62 (RESTYLED)

$3404., and up, f.o.b.
260 to 345 HP (THROUGH '69)

new UPRIGHT GRILLE with "OLDSMOBILE" NAME ABOVE

new SIDE SCULPTURING

(CONT'D.)

SUPER 88

98

HOLIDAY SPORTS SED. 98)

98 WHEEL COVERS

62 (CONT'D.) STARFIRE

new HARDTOP CPE. IN STARFIRE SERIES

$3423., and up, f.o.b.

63

DYNAMIC 88

DYNAMIC 88 CONVERT. AVAIL.

(CONT'D.)

260

OLDSMOBILE

SU-88 GRILLE LIKE DYNAMIC 88

SUPER 88

SU-88 FIESTA

63 (CONT'D.)

STARFIRE REAR ROOFLINE

STARFIRE

STARFIRE REAR

STARFIRE WHEEL COVER

98 TOWN SEDAN

98-LS (LUXURY SEDAN)

(98 DETAILS)

4-DR. H/T $4238., f.o.b.

There's 'Something Extra' about owning an

OLDSMOBILE

NINETY-EIGHT · SUPER 88 · DYNAMIC 88 · F-85 · STARFIRE · JETFIRE

$3391.,
f.o.b.
Jetstar 88
New full-size "88" series at a new lower price!
'64 OLDS
WHERE THE ACTION IS!
new 330-cubic-inch Jetfire Rocket V-8
JETSTAR 88 CELEBRITY SEDAN
JETSTAR 88 HOLIDAY SEDAN
Jetstar 88
FIESTA STATION WAGON (2- or 3-seat)
DYNAMIC 88 HOLIDAY COUPE
CELEBRITY SEDAN
SUPER 88
DYNAMIC 88
394-cubic-inch
Starfire V-8 Engine
J 1964
Brilliant new sports coupe in the medium-price class!
Jetstar I
TOWN SEDAN
64
Starfire
98
S-1964
NINETY-EIGHT
1964
Ninety Eight
J-64
REAR
FENDER
(98)

65

330 CID V8   260 HP   123" WB
7.75 x 14 TIRES

Jetstar 88 $3334.,
f.o.b.

DYNAMIC 88 LINE
JOINED BY
new DELTA 88 →

Delta 88.

$3697.,
f.o.b.

8.25 x 14
TIRES

$3504.,
f.o.b.
DYNAMIC
88
H/T

123"
WB

425 CID
SUPER
ROCKET
V8
360 HP
(to 370 in DELTA 88)

DELTA 88 DASH

new GRILLE

OLDSMOBILE

note THAT STARFIRE and 98
have OWN GRILLE
DESIGNS

CVT.

370 HP
STARFIRE →

H/T

$4761.,
f.o.b.

98 (126" WB)

$4237.,
f.o.b.

98
LUXURY
SEDAN

$4334.,
f.o.b.

Ninety-Eight

WITH
VINYL
TOP ↓

8.55 x 14 TIRES

HOLIDAY
SPORT
SEDAN

NINETY-EIGHT

98 DASH

263

'65 OLDSMOBILE
The Rocket Action Car!

PACKARD
(1899-1958)
PACKARD MOTOR CAR CO., DETROIT

DETAILS OF COWL VENT, ETC.

SIX-CYL. OR STRAIGHT-8 L-HEAD ENGS.

110 SIX $975.

INTERIOR DETAILS

40
(1800 SERIES)

120 EIGHT $1095.

CVT.

$867 TO $6300 delivered in Detroit, State taxes extra. Prices subject to change without notice.

Air Cool-ditioning is available on closed models of the Packard 120, Super-Eight 160, and Custom Super-Eight 180 at extra cost, installed at the factory.

AIR CONDITIONING INTRODUCED FOR FIRST TIME!

OVERDRIVE OPTIONAL

ASK THE MAN WHO OWNS ONE

GRILLE GUARD ON 160 AND LARGER MODELS

160 SUPER 8 and ENGINE

Model illustrated is Packard Super-8 One-Sixty Touring Sedan $1632 (white sidewall tires extra)*

(CONTINUED)

PACKARD

40 (CONT'D.)

DARRIN SEDAN — 138" WB — $6100.
THIS DARRIN MODEL (RARE) has TOP and BODY DESIGN ENTIRELY DIFFERENT FROM OTHER PACKARDS

180 CUSTOM 8 BY DARRIN — 4570. — 127" WB
DARRIN CONVERTIBLE

LIMOUSINE

180 CUSTOM 8 FORMAL SEDAN — $2825.

HEADLIGHTS SUNK DEEPER INTO FENDERS, with PARKING LIGHTS SET ON TOP
$1436. $1024.

120 WAGON

DLX. SEDAN INTERIOR (110)

110 SIX

new 1-PIECE BACKLIGHT

DASH

"the Class of '41"
41 (1900 SERIES)

6 lines of cars — 41 body styles
$907 TO $5550

261 AVAIL. TRIM COMBINATIONS!

120

180 DARRIN

265

PACKARD — new CLIPPER 8 CYL. (STARTS 4-41)

41½ (1951 SERIES) $1375.

OTHER 1941 MODELS CONTINUE ALSO

Clipper — new 2-DR. CLIPPERS NOW ALSO AVAIL.

110
180

INTERIOR

LOOKING AHEAD? SKIPPER THE CLIPPER

42-45 (2000 SERIES)

new CHOICE of 6 or 8-CYL. CLIPPERS

ELECTROMATIC DRIVE
SIMPLIFIED DRIVING WITH NO JERK - NO SLIP - NO CREEP

CUSTOM SUPER CLIPPER

SUPER 8 has 148" WB

$1746. DELUXE CLIPPER

46-47 (2100 SERIES)

(BIG CITY PACKARD SHOWROOMS MORE LUXURIOUS THAN THIS RURAL OUTLET)

266

$3161.
STATION SEDAN (new)

EIGHT

NEW SMOOTH SIDE BODIES

← SUPER-8 CVT. IS FIRST OF 1948 PACKARDS TO BE INTRODUCED.

$2990.

SUPER 8 130 HP

$2529.

EARLY
48-49
(RESTYLED) (2200 SERIES)

$3461. CUSTOM 8 160 HP

$3866.
127" WB

1948 - EARLY '49 DASH ILLUSTR. ON NEXT PAGE

CUSTOM 8 has CRISS-CROSS PIECES IN GRILLE.

ASK THE MAN WHO OWNS ONE

267

Packard

CLOSE-UP VIEW OF DASH (2200 SERIES)

135 HP (8)
150 HP (SU.8)
160 HP (CUST. 8)

$2383. ('50)

DELUXE 8

EIGHT (120" WB)

SUPER 8 new 127" WB

DASH and BACKLIGHT DETAILS

Ultramatic Drive AVAIL.

CUSTOM 8 127" WB

"Golden Anniversary" MODELS — new LARGER BACKLIGHTS ON 4-DOOR SEDANS

49½-50
(2300 SERIES)
77 MAJOR IMPROVEMENTS

"NEW, ALL-NEW"

PRICE RANGE $2302. TO $3797.

200 (145 HP)

Prestige car of the medium-priced field: Packard '200' Club Sedan—$2366
—one of nine exciting new models for '51
122" WB

250 CVT.

51-52
(2500 SER.)

(TOTALLY RESTYLED 2400 SERIES)

300

250 MAYFAIR

REAR SIDE DETAILS

1952 MODEL (left) SIMILAR, BUT has new HOOD ORNAMENT and MEDALLION ON GRILLE

400 PATRICIAN

COSTLY MODELS continue CORMORANT FIGURE as 1951 ORNAMENT

1951 MODELS have "PACKARD" NAME ABOVE GRILLE

New Armor-rib body construction!
New Tele-glance instrument panel!
New Safeti-set brake!

—the one for '51!

269

$2588.

CLIPPER DELUXE

New Packard CLIPPER

160 HP

new HOOD ORNAMENT and SMOOTH HORIZONTAL GRILLE PIECE (ON CLIPPER ONLY)

53 (2600 SERIES)

CLIPPER SERIES RETURNS (PREVIOUSLY AVAIL. 1941-1947)

new CAVALIER 127" WB

$3234.

MAYFAIR

MAYFAIR H/T ALSO, W/O 3 CHROME REAR FENDER PLAQUES SEEN ON ABOVE CVT.

400 PATRICIAN

new GROOVES IN HORIZONTAL GRILLE PIECE (EXCEPT ON CLIPPER)

$5209.

new CARIBBEAN

270

PANAMA

CLIPPER DELUXE

SUPER CLIPPER

122", 127" OR 149" WB
150, 165, 185 OR 212 HP

54
(5400 SERIES)

DASH

CAVALIER

PATRICIAN

FINAL STRAIGHT-8 ENGINES
(288, 327 OR 359 CID)

STUDEBAKER-PACKARD MERGER

122" WB

CLIPPER

FIRST MAJOR RESTYLING SINCE 1951

new V8 ENG. with O.H.V.
(320 OR 352 CID)

PATRICIAN

PRICE RANGE:
$2586. TO $5932.

225, 245 OR 260 HP @ 4600 RPM

55
(5500 SERIES)

127" WB

400

CARIBBEAN

271

PACKARD

2731. CLIPPER DELUXE

CLIPPER SUPER also avail.

$3069.

CUSTOM CLIPPER

CUSTOM CLIPPER CONSTELLATION H/T
3164.

MEMBERS of CLIPPER GRILLE NOW HORIZONTAL.

122" WB (CLIPPERS) OTHERS, 127" WB

56
(5600 SERIES)

new DISPLACEMENT OF 374 CID ON ALL PACKARD V8 ENGINES. ALL BUT CARIBBEAN have 290 HP @ 4600 RPM.

3483.

EXECUTIVE

H/T $3658.

WIDER-SPACED GRILLE PIECES with MESH BACKGROUND

$4160.

PATRICIAN

$4190.
400
H/T

"ASK THE MAN WHO OWNS the New ONE"

$5995.

CARIBBEAN has 310 HP @ 4600 RPM

272

57 PACKARD (57-L SERIES) new 120½" WB

$3212.

CLIPPER

new SMALLER DISPLACEMENT OF 289 CID

HP REDUCED TO 275 @ 4800 RPM

SEDAN and WAGON are ONLY CHOICES LISTED DURING 1957.

new 116½" BODIES LIKE STUDEBAKER (THROUGH '58)

275 HP (THROUGH '58)

WAGON

$3384. (AS IN '57)

ENG. SPECS. AS IN 1957.

58 (58-L SERIES) THE FINAL PACKARDS

See the all-new '58 Packards:
- The panoramic Packard Hardtop
- The supercharged Packard Hawk
- The luxurious Packard 4-door Sedan
- The versatile Packard Station Wagon

Studebaker-Packard CORPORATION
Where pride of Workmanship comes first!

SEDAN

FRONT END DETAILS

new HAWK H/T

4 HEADLIGHTS (EXCEPT ON HAWK)

HAWK has 2 HEADLIGHTS, LOWER GRILLE

$3995.

PLAYBOY 48

48 HP with 133 CID HERCULES ENGINE OR 40 HP with 91 CID CONT. ENG.

STEEL RETRACTABLE TOP

97 BLT. 4 CYL.

PLAYBOY MOTOR CAR CORP., BUFFALO, N.Y. (1946-1951)

3.73 OR 4.1 GEAR RATIO 90" W.B.

$985.

INTER.

PLYMOUTH DIVISION
CHRYSLER
CORPORATION

Plymouth (SINCE JUNE, 1928)

DASH

6 CYLINDERS
(SINCE 1933)

new 117½" WB
(THROUGH 1948)
6.00 × 16 TIRES (TO 1947)

new 1-PIECE
REAR WINDOW

2-DR.

ROAD KING

WAGON

COUPE

201.3 CID
(SINCE '34)

DE LUXE

new
84 HP @ 3600 RPM
(87 HP with
ALUMINUM
CYL. HEAD)

new
ROTARY DOOR LATCHES

WIPERS NOW
FASTENED
BELOW
WINDSHIELD

CVT.

40

P-9 ROAD KING
P-10 DE LUXE

PLYMOUTH
BUILDS GREAT CARS

COUPES START AT $645 | SEDANS START AT $699
DELIVERED IN DETROIT, MICH.

ROAD KING MODELS DO NOT
HAVE ADDITIONAL ROTATING
VENT-WINDOWS IN
FRONT
DOORS.

SEDAN

new GRILLE
and SEALED-BEAM
HEADLIGHTS

Plymouth

DE LUXE

SPEC. DLX.

$685. AND UP **41**

P-11 DE LUXE
P-12 SPECIAL DE LUXE

2 VIEWS OF DASH

87 OR 92 HP @ 3800 RPM

"BUY WISELY — BUY PLYMOUTH THE CAR THAT STANDS UP BEST"

new CLUB COUPE (5-PASS.)

4-DR., 5-WINDOW TOWN SEDAN ('42 only)

95 HP @ 3400 RPM

(RESTYLED)

42

P-14C SPEC. DLX.

P-14S DE LUXE

FRONT DETAIL

275

Plymouth

SPECIAL DE LUXE *has* CHROME EFFECT ON WINDSHIELD FRAME

1946 *has* FLAT BUTTON TYPE DOOR LOCK COVERS.

1948 *has new* 7.50 × 15 LOW-PRESSURE TIRES.

46-48*

P-15S DLX. OR P-15C SPECIAL DLX.

* = CONT'D. TO 2-49

95 HP @ 3600 RPM

CLUB COUPE

$1075. TO $2068.
(PRICE RANGE, 1946 TO EARLY 1949)

CONVERTIBLE DASH IS PAINTED IN BODY COLOR, INSTEAD OF BEING WOODGRAINED.

REAR (SEDAN)

SEDAN INTERIOR

SPECIAL DE LUXE *has* RADIO GRILLE

DE LUXE

Plymouth

new ALL-METAL 2-DR. SUBURBAN WAGON
P-17

SEDAN REAR DOORS NOW FRONT-HINGED

6.40 x 15 OR 6.70 x 15 TIRES (THROUGH '52)

SPECIAL DELUXE 4-DOOR WAGON has WOODEN PANELS.
P-18

97 HP @ 3600 RPM (THROUGH '52)

CLUB COUPE

new "Double-Size" CVT. BACKLIGHT has REMOVABLE, ZIPPERED CENTER SECTION

49

P-17 (111" WB)
P-18 (118½" WB)

(TOTALLY RESTYLED)

HORIZONTAL CREASES ON BUMPERS ('49 ONLY)

new SWITCH-KEY STARTING

SLOGAN: "The car that likes to be compared"

277

Plymouth

DE LUXE

3-WINDOW BUSINESS COUPE

SPECIAL DE LUXE

PRICE RANGE: $1371. TO $2372.

P-19 DE LUXE (111" WB)
P-20 DE LUXE; SPEC. DLX. (118½" WB)

50

new EMBLEM

DASH

new SMOOTH BUMPER SURFACE

new GRILLE has FEWER PIECES.

278

Plymouth

P-22 CONCORD

111" WB

1951 MODELS ILLUSTRATED UNLESS OTHERWISE NOTED.

1951 BELVEDERE is new H/T.

SHIELD BADGE REPLACED BY CIRCLE ON '52.

MODEL NAME IN SCRIPT ON 1952 FRONT FENDER

P-23 CAMBRIDGE and CRANBRK. have 118½" WB

51-52

new CONCORD, CAMBRIDGE, CRANBROOK MODEL NAMES

('51) DASH

'50 PLYMOUTH TAXI

1952 BELVEDERE (BELOW) has new REAR COLOR SWEEP

('52)

Plymouth

100 HP @ 3600 RPM

SAVOY WAGON

CRANBROOK BELVEDERE

new SPORT WIRE WHEELS OPTIONAL

53
(TOTALLY RESTYLED)
P-24-1 CAMBRIDGE
P-24-2 CRANBR.

CRANBROOK

new 114" WB (THROUGH '54)

6.70 x 15 TIRES (TO '56)

P-25-3 BELVEDERE

P-25-1 PLAZA

LATE '54 has new 230.2 CID and 110 HP @ 3600 RPM

P-25-2 SAVOY

$1618. UP

54

EARLY 1954 BELVEDERE H/T DOES NOT HAVE THIS COLOR BAND ON SIDE

BELVEDERE

280

Plymouth

230 CID 6 CYL. OR new 241 CID or 260 CID V8s.

new AUTOMATIC TRANSMISSION CONTROL on DASH

PLAZA

SAVOY

PRICED FROM $1639.

55

6 = 117 HP @ 4000 RPM

V8 = 157 or 167 HP @ 4400 RPM

(TOTALLY RESTYLED with new "FORWARD LOOK")

new 115" WB (THROUGH '56)

CLUB COUPE

new PANORAMIC WINDSHIELD

BELVEDERE

H/T

6-CYL. has STRAIGHT EMBLEM ABOVE GRILLE →

new FRENCHED HEADLIGHTS

V8 has ABOVE TYPE of EMBLEM

281

Plymouth

SUBURBAN

6.70 × 15 TIRES
(ALL BUT new FURY)

CUSTOM SUBURBAN

PLAZA

SPORT SUBURBAN

BELVEDERE
SEDAN (ABOVE)
4-DR. H/T (BELOW)

PUSHBUTTON POWERFLITE

56 P-28 (6)
P-29 (V8)

125, 180, 187, 200, 240 OR 270 HP

SAVOY

H/T

new **Fury** (WITH 303 CID V8)
7.10 × 15 TIRES)

← new SHARPLY-PEAKED TAIL FINS

new MESH AT GRILLE CENTER

1956

282

Plymouth

PLAZA

EARLY '57 (6 OPEN SLOTS BELOW BUMPERS)

BELVEDERE

SAVOY

BELVEDERE

LATE '57 (EXTRA VERTICAL MEMBERS BELOW BUMPERS)

318 CID V8 IN FURY

new 118" WB (122" WB ON WAGONS) (THROUGH '61)

new 8.00 × 14 TIRES ON FURY H/T

SPORT SDN. (BELV.)

TAILGATE WINDOW DETAILS

SECRET LUGGAGE COMPARTMENT. Almost 10 cubic feet of locked space for safe, out-of-sight storage of luggage, cameras and other valuables. On all 6-pass. models.

132, 197, 215, 235 OR 290 HP

new 7.50 × 14 TIRES (ALL BUT FURY)

57

(TOTALLY RESTYLED)

P-30 (6)
P-31 (V8)

$1899. UP

DASH

283

Plymouth

58
LP-1 (6)
LP-2 (V8)

The De Luxe Suburban—2-door, 6-passenger
The Custom Suburban—2-door, 6-passenger
The Custom Suburban—4-door, 9- or 6-passenger

The Plaza 2-door Business Coupe
The Savoy 4-door Sedan
The Savoy 4-door Hardtop
The Belvedere 4-door Sedan
The Belvedere Convertible

SPORT SUBURBAN

★ Star of the Forward Look

INSTRUMENT CLUSTER

4 HEADLIGHTS

7.50 × 14 TIRES (8.00 × 14 on 9-PASS. WAGONS and FURY H/T)

BELVEDERE

FURY

230 CID 6 (132 HP @ 3600)
318 CID V8 (225 or 250 HP @ 4400)
350 CID V8 (305 or 315 HP @ 5000 RPM)

newest engine—"Golden Commando V-8"
(WITH ELECTRONIC FUEL INJECTION)

SILVER SPECIAL (RARE!)
(PLAZA)

284

Plymouth

CUSTOM SUBURBAN

SAVOY — 4-door Sedan, V-8 or 6

BELVEDERE — 2-door Sedan, V-8 or 6

59
MP-1 (6)
MP-2 (V8)

7.50 x 14 TIRES

OPTIONAL new SWIVEL SEATS (STD. IN SPORT FURY)

DASH

SPORT SUBURBAN

new SPORT FURY H/T

FINAL USE OF L-HEAD DESIGN IN PLYMOUTH SIX

new "CONTINENTAL BULGE" ON DECK LID

FURY

230 CID 6 (132 HP @ 3600)
318 CID V8 (230 or 260 HP @ 4400 RPM)
361 CID V8 (305 HP @ 4600 RPM)

Plymouth

SAVOY

BELVEDERE

new SLANTING O.H.V. 225 CID 6 (145 HP @ 4000 RPM) (TO '71)

V8s have 318, 361, OR 383 CID (230, 260, 305, 310, 325 OR 330 HP)

note THE REAR FENDER ORNAMENTS WHICH IDENTIFY EACH INDIVIDUAL MODEL SERIES.

CUSTOM SUBURBAN

FURY

4-DR. H/T

2-DR. H/T

WITH GRILLE GUARD

WITH SEMI-RECTANGULAR STEERING WHEEL

WITHOUT GRILLE GUARD

60
PP-1 (6 CYL.)
PP-2 (V8)

SHOWN with ROUND STEERING WHEEL

DASH

7.50 x 14 TIRES

CLOSER DETAILS OF WAGON

286

Plymouth

7.00 × 14 TIRES (6)
7.50 × 14 ON 6-CYL. WAGONS and V8s.
8.00 × 14 ON 9-PASS. V8 WAGON

Battery-saving Alternator keeps battery charged when generators can't. Many police and taxi fleets pay extra to get special Alternator installations. Yet the amazing new Alternator is standard equipment on all 1961 Chrysler Corporation cars.

PLYMOUTH — This car traveled 328 miles without a battery. Alternator, standard on 1961 Chrysler Corporation cars, provided all necessary electrical energy.

61
RP-1 (6)
RP-2 (V8)

SPT. SBN.

$2260. UP

FURY

145 TO 375 HP

LARGEST OF 4 PLYMOUTH V8s IS *new* 413 CID ENGINE (UP TO 375 HP @ 5200 RPM)

118" WB (WAGONS 122")

GRILLE GUARD AVAIL. ON SOME 1961 MODELS

new GRILLE   287   ...SOLID BEAUTY

Plymouth

Look at Plymouth now!

SAVOY

PRICED FROM $2531.

SAVOY

6 = 6.50 × 14 TIRES
V8 = 7.00 × 14

BELVEDERE

Plymouth Belvedere 2-dr Sedan

'62

SP-1 (6)
SP-2 (V8)

(TOTALLY RESTYLED)

new 116" WB

New Forward Flair Design

FURY

FURY

145 TO 410 HP

TURBO-FURY (SPECIAL)

Special red, white and blue insignia, new wheel covers and new rear deck design tell you that this one is the real thing! There is no mistaking a new Sport Fury—hardtop or convertible.

Action! Fly to 60 mph in 8.5 secs. with optional 305-hp Golden Commando V-8 engine.

NEW SPORT FURY

288

Plymouth

SAVOY

BELVEDERE

7.00 x 14 TIRES

FURY

V8 OPTIONS

318 CID (230 HP @ 4400)
361 CID (265 HP @ 4400)
383 CID (320 to 330 HP)
426 CID (370 HP @ 4600 to 425 HP @ 5600 RPM)

FURY

FURY

1963 IS ONLY YEAR with UNUSUAL FRONT CORNER PARK./DIRECTIONAL LIGHTS

with a 5-year or 50,000-mile warranty

63

TP-1 (6 CYL.)
TP-2 (V8)

new GRILLE
new TAIL-LIGHTS
new FULL-LENGTH SIDE TRIM

Get up and go Plymouth!

new 426 CID V8 ENGINE KNOWN AS "Super Stock"

DASH

A	Transmission Drive Selector (optional)	G	Defroster Outlets
B	Transmission Parking Lock	H	Windshield Wiper Control
C	Clock (optional)	I	Ignition Switch
D	Turn Signal Indicator	J	Cigarette Lighter
E	Heater Controls (optional)	K	Ash Receiver
F	Headlights and Panel Lights	L	Glove Compartment Lock
		M	Radio (optional)

SPORT FURY

PLYMOUTH'S ON THE MOVE

Plymouth

Savoy 2-Door Sedan

SAVOY

Savoy 6- or 9-Passenger Station Wagon

7.00 × 14 TIRES

BELVEDERE

318, 361, 383 and 426 CID V8s

FURY

230 to 425 HP

64

VP-1 (6 CYL.)
(V8) VP-2

FURY wagon

REAR OF FURY WAGON

$3195.

SPORT FURY

new H/T ROOFLINE

new CONVEX GRILLE

Plymouth

BELVEDERE II 116" WB

Belvedere Satellite

Belvedere I

new BELVEDERE SATELLITE IS AVAIL. WITH TOP-OF-LINE 426 CID V8 WITH 425 HP @ 6000 RPM.

BELV. has 7.35 × 14 TIRES (EXC. WAGON)

Fury I

273 CID BARRACUDA V8 ENG. NOW AVAIL. IN BELVEDERE I (180 HP @ 4200 RPM)

PACE CAR AT 1965 INDY 500 RACE

SPORT FURY

Fury II

7.75 × 14 TIRES
8.55 × 14 (FURY WAGON)

DASH

Fury III

FURY III

145 to 425 HP

65

AR-1 (6-CYL.)
AR-2 (V8)

ALL FURY TYPES GET new 119" WB (WAGONS 121")

Fury III 4-Door Hardtop

THE ROARING '65s

291

PONTIAC MOTOR DIVISION of
GENERAL MOTORS CORPORATION

Pontiac
AMERICA'S FINEST LOW-PRICED CAR

SINCE 1926

6.00 x 16 TIRES (SINCE '35; 6-CYL.)

SPECIAL 6

AMERICA'S FINEST LOW-PRICED CAR

Pontiac's sealed chassis is where Pontiac's amazing durability begins. Rugged, powerful, yet with micrometric precision in every vital unit, the Pontiac chassis is engineered to serve well long past the point when the average car is past its prime.

BUILT TO LAST 100,000 MILES

40

DELUXE 6

SPECIAL 6

DELUXE 8

TORPEDO 8

"Silver Streak" CHROME STRIPS ALONG HOOD, REAR DECK, A PONTIAC CHARACTERISTIC SINCE 1935.

ONLY $783* FOR THE SPECIAL SIX BUSINESS COUPE
OTHER MODELS SLIGHTLY HIGHER

"HA" SPECIAL 6 MODEL 25 has 117" WB

"HB" DELUXE 6 MODEL 26 and "HA" DLX. 8 MODEL 28 have 120" WB

"HB" TORPEDO 8 MODEL 29 has 122" WB

TRIPLE-TIERED BUMPER GUARD AVAIL. ALSO

A-11214 1940

292

Pontiac Torpedoes

PONTIAC PRICES BEGIN AT $828* FOR DE LUXE "TORPEDO" SIX BUSINESS COUPE

CUSTOM TORPEDO

STREAMLINER TORPEDO

DELUXE TORPEDO

CUSTOM TORPEDO

[ONLY $25 MORE FOR AN EIGHT IN ANY MODEL!]

41

NEW INTERIOR LUXURY is exemplified by this attractive new 1941 Pontiac instrument panel. Electric clock (except on some models) and radio at extra cost.

THE FINE CAR *Pontiac* WITH THE LOW PRICE

DETAILS OF new GRILLE and EMBLEM

293

Pontiac

Torpedo Business Coupe
Torpedo Sport Coupe
Torpedo Two-Door Sedan
Torpedo Sedan Coupe
Torpedo Metropolitan Four-Door Sedan
Torpedo Convertible Sedan Coupe
Torpedo Four-Door Sedan
Streamliner Four-Door Sedan
Streamliner Station Wagon

42-45

ONLY $25 MORE FOR AN EIGHT IN ANY MODEL

$895.
and up

"with the things you've always liked — AND 15 NEW ONES TOO!"

THE **FINE** CAR WITH THE **LOW** PRICE
Streamliner Sedan Coupe

Pontiac offers ten new models superior in 15 ways to last year's

Full Speed Ahead on National Defense

To the production of a new type of heavy machine gun for the United States Navy, Pontiac is devoting two entire plants, totaling 10 acres of floor space and staffed with thousands of Pontiac production experts and skilled craftsmen working three shifts a day. In addition Pontiac has a total of 223 sub-contractors supplying machines and material to build this new gun which naval authorities describe as "the most effective weapon of its size ever produced." Defense comes first at Pontiac—and Pontiac is going full speed ahead!

Pontiac

Pontiac

Finest of the Famous "Silver Streaks"

TORPEDO

STREAMLINER

46

WHAT'S NEW AND IMPROVED IN THE 1946 PONTIAC

New, beautiful exterior appearance... New instrument panel... Heavier chrome finish... Improved, rust-resistant bodies... New interior trim... Improved clutch... New, wider wheel rims... Longer-life muffler and tail pipe... Improved cooling.

STREAMLINER **TORPEDO**

47

NO VERTICAL PIECES IN 1947 GRILLE

TORPEDO **TORPEDO DELUXE**

48

STREAMLINER DE LUXE

DE LUXE MODELS *have* CHROME STRIP *on* SIDE *of* FRONT FENDER, *and* CHROME REAR FENDER PADS

PONTIAC

49
(TOTALLY RESTYLED)

ALL-STEEL WAGON

50
VERTICAL "TEETH" NOW ADDED TO UPPER SECTION OF GRILLE

WHEEL COVER

296

REAR FENDER PAD DETAILS

51

L-HEAD 6 CYL. and STRAIGHT-8 ENGINES CONTINUE (THROUGH '54)

('52)

Dollar for Dollar you can't beat a
Pontiac

1952 WHEEL COVER

52

SIDE VIEW OF MASCOT

New High-Performance Economy Axle

More Power

new SIDE TRIM

New *Dual-Range*
Hydra-Matic Drive*

PONTIAC

CHIEFTAN SPECIAL

new "DUAL STREAK" RESTYLING FEATURES TWIN GROUPS of CHROME BANDS ALONG HOOD and DECK, with new BODIES

CHIEFTAN DELUXE

new 53 1-PIECE WINDSHIELD

WAGONS with GRAIN-DECORATED UPPER PANELS (ABOVE) ARE PRICED $80. ABOVE SIMILAR WAGONS of ONE SOLID COLOR ONLY.

new 122" WB

$1956.

$2774.

PRICE RANGE

The experimental Parisienne stands only 56 inches high. Inside and out it is a designer's dream of how one "car of the future" might be styled and equipped.

PARISIENNE (SHOW CAR) PUBLICLY DISPLAYED, BUT NOT A PRODUCTION BODY TYPE

De Luxe Catalina

Dollar for Dollar you can't beat a

Pontiac

298

PONTIAC

CHIEFTAN SPECIAL 6
(ALSO AVAIL. as 8)

CHIEFTAN DELUXE
(6 OR 8 CYL.)

A BRIEF (1 YR.) RETURN TO SINGLE GROUP OF CHROME STRIPS ON HOOD and DECK

54

new GRILLE with EMBLEM PLACED ABOVE

STAR CHIEF CUSTOM 8
(AT RIGHT and BELOW)

THE NEW *Star Chief*

8-CYL. SERIES IDENTIFIED BY THESE "STARS" ON SIDE OF REAR FENDER

STAR CHIEF DE LUXE 8 (BELOW) COSTS LESS THAN CUSTOM 8

CVT.

FRONT END and WHEEL COVER DETAILS

299

PONTIAC

Pontiac leads in station wagon value with four models — the beautiful 860, left, in two- and four-door models, the spectacular 870 four-door and the fabulous Safari.

CHIEFTAN 860

(TOTALLY RESTYLED)
55

new PANORAMIC WINDSHIELD

CHIEFTAN 870

CHIEFTAN = 122" WB
STAR CHIEF = 124" WB

CHIEFTAN 870 CATALINA H/T (2 VIEWS)

new DASH

PRICE RANGE: $2105. TO $3128.

ALL MODELS with new "STRATO-STREAK" O.H.V. V8 ENGINE — 180 OR 200 HP

new STAR CHIEF CUST. SAFARI 2 DR. LUXURY WAGON

Pontiac's flair for years-ahead styling was never more evident than in the fabulous all-new Safari.

STAR CHIEF CUSTOM CATALINA (CVT. ALSO AVAIL.)

DUMPER GUARDS AVAILABLE (RARE)

300

CHIEFTAN

SAFARI

STAR CHIEF

new 4-DR. H/T

56 Pontiac

TO 227 HP

STAR CHIEF *Custom Convertible*

PLASTIC "JR. STAR CHIEF" CHILD'S ELECTRIC CARS ALSO, FOR DEALER PROMOTIONAL PURPOSES

REAR DETAILS

301

PONTIAC

CHIEFTAN 252 HP

SUPER CHIEF 270 HP

STAR CHIEF 270 HP

SAFARI WAGON

57

SU. CHIEF WAGON DOOR

BONNEVILLE (new) (LIMITED PRODUCTION)

STAR CHIEF has HEAVY CHROME BAND PLACED WITHIN COLOR CONTRAST PANEL ON REAR FENDER

AMERICA'S NUMBER 1 ROAD CAR!

new FRONT END (NO LONGER USES "SILVER STREAK" CHROME BANDS)

STAR CH. 2-DR. H/T

302

PONTIAC CHIEFTAN

3 STAR-LIKE FIGS. ON REAR FENDER OF CHIEFTAN; 4 ON SUPER CHIEF. (EACH MODEL CAN BE IDENTIFIED BY FENDER DECOR., AS ILLUS. BELOW)

SUPER CHIEF

58 (RESTYLED)

STAR CHIEF

BOLDEST ADVANCE IN 50 YEARS

BOLD NEW Bonneville BY PONTIAC

PACE CAR AT 1958 INDY 500 RACE

BONNEVILLE

303

PONTIAC

CATALINA

new "WIDE-TRACK"
59
(TOTALLY RESTYLED)

122" WB (CATALINA SERIES and on BONNEVL. WAGON)
124" WB ON OTHERS

new BONNEVILLE VISTA 4-DR. H/T

"BONNEVILLE" NAME ON BONNEVL. GRILLE

CATALINA SAFARI WAGON

(WIDTH EXAGGERATED)

"PONTIAC" NAME ON GRILLE OF CATALINA and STAR CHIEF. STAR CHIEF has STAR-LIKE FIGURES ALONG SIDE OF REAR FENDER.

DASH

8.00 x 14 TIRES

245 HP (280 w. Hydra Matic)
BONNEVL. has 260 HP (300 w. Hyd.)

304

PONTIAC 1960

STAR CHIEF

THE ONLY CAR WITH WIDE-TRACK WHEELS

WAGON AND VISTA DETAILS

BONNEVILLE

60

VENTURA HT

CATALINA 2-DR.

SAFARI

61 (RESTYLED)

BONNEVILLE (STAR CHF. TAILLIGHTS SIMILAR)

305

PONTIAC

STAR CHIEF

61 CONT'D.

BONNEVILLE OFTEN *has* "BONNEVILLE" NAME ON GRILLE AS ILLUSTR.

VISTA 4 DOOR HARDTOPS

STAR CHIEF

STAR CHIEF VISTA

Wide-Track Pontiac
WIDEST STANCE ON THE ROAD

62

Bonneville

CATALINA

CATALINA 9-PASSENGER SAFARI

(CONTINUED)

STRATO-CHIEF
(SOLD ONLY IN CANADA)

WAGONS

LAURENTIAN
2-DOOR

PONTIAC

LAURENTIAN
(SOLD ONLY IN CANADA)

62 (CONT'D.)

SPORT COUPE

SPORT COUPES

PARISIENNE
(SOLD ONLY IN CANADA)
SEDAN

GP

GRAND PRIX
New DETAILS

MANUAL SHIFT CONSOLE
BUCKET SEATS
TACH.
AUTO. SHIFT CONSOLE

303 HP
4 BBL. CARB.
$3917.

307

CATALINA
9-PASSENGER SAFARI

STAR CHIEF 4-DOOR SEDAN

PONTIAC

CATALINA SPORTS SEDAN

BONNEVILLE SPORTS COUPE

BONNEVILLE VISTA

CATALINA / ST. CHIEF

CATALINA

BONNEVILLE

63

2 VIEWS OF G.P.

GP PONTIAC GRAND PRIX

'63 WIDE-TRACK PONTIAC

308

PONTIAC 120" WB CATALINA

STAR CHIEF
(FRONT SIMILAR TO CATALINA)
123" WB
235 HP

64

CATALINA SEDAN

BONNEVILLE

WHEEL COVER

123" WB

BONN. BROUGHAM w. VINYL TOP (BELOW)

INTERIOR

$3995.
(CVT.)

306 H.P.

PRESTON CLOTH-and-MORROKIDE INTERIOR

WAGON
(BONNEVILLE)

G.P.

120" WB

309

PONTIAC

CATALINA

CATALINA 2+2

note LOUVRES ON COWL OF 2+2

BON. BROUGHAM INTERIOR

BONNEVILLE

BONNEVILLE BROUGHAM 4-DR. H/T (325 HP)

65

G.P.

CAT. 2+2 INTERIOR

Pontiac for 1965
The year of the Quick Wide-Tracks

new GRILLE

Grand Prix

310

(1947-1949)

PUP 48-49

PUP MOTOR CAR CO., SPENCER, WIS.

1 OR 2 CYL., 7½ OR 10 HP

REAR ENGINE

AT NASH DEALERS

Rambler 6 CYL.

TOP DOWN
TOP UP

$1808., f.o.b. (CVT. OR WAGON)

100" WB
82 HP

MODEL 5021
New Rambler Convertible Landau
(CUSTOM SERIES)

50

"RAMBLER" NAME REVIVED BY NASH FOR THIS NEW COMPACT SERIES. CVT. INTRO. 3-50; WAGON 5-50

51-52

new "SUPER"

MODEL 5127 (5227) "COUNTRY CLUB" HARDTOP INTRO. 6-51

SUBURBAN MODEL 5114 (5214)

57,555 RAMBLERS BLT. 1951; 53,055 RAMBLERS SOLD IN 1952

FIRST 2 DIGITS OF MODEL NUMBER INDICATE YEAR OF CAR

CONVERTIBLE CONTINUES

RAMBLER

85 HP (90 with Hydra-Matic)

5321 CVT. — CUSTOM

53

5327 COUNTRY CLUB H/T

GREENBRIER

SUPER 2-DR. SUBURBAN IS LOWEST-PRICED: $2003., f.o.b.

5406 CLUB SEDAN — new DE LUXE

SUPER

5417

5414

$1550., f.o.b.

54 100" and 108" WB

Nash Motors, Division of
AMERICAN MOTORS CORP.
DETROIT, MICH.

5425

5427

CUSTOM

note LUGGAGE RACK AND DIP IN REAR ROOFLINE

REAR DETAILS (CROSS-COUNTRY)

new 4-DR. "CROSS-COUNTRY" WAGON (5428)

312

RAMBLER a Whole **New Idea** in Automobiles

DELUXE 5515

5514

SUPER

NEW IDEA! *Touch this knob—and it will always be springtime in your Rambler. No cold in winter! No heat in summer! No dust or traffic roar! You breathe only fresh, filtered air. It's American Motors' All-Season Air Conditioning*—greatest health, comfort, safety feature of fifty years. Needs no trunk space. And you buy a Rambler so equipped for less than the price of an ordinary car!*
*Patents applied for

PRICES START AT
$1585.,
f.o.b.
(DLX. 2-DR.)

5517
COUNTRY
CLUB
CUSTOM

ON 9-22-55, FINAL AMC CAR ASSEMBLED AT EL SEGUNDO, CALIF. BRANCH FACTORY, with "DC-" SERIAL NUMBERS. KENOSHA, WIS. FACTORY CONTINUES with "D-" SERIAL NUMBERS AS USUAL.

new GRILLE with CRISS-CROSS PIECES

83,852 BLT.

55

INTERIOR (H/T)

CROSS-COUNTRY 5518

HUDSON RAMBLER

NASH RAMBLER

(DETERMINE BY NAME-PLATE ON GRILLE)

NOW AT *Nash* DEALERS AND HUDSON DEALERS EVERYWHERE

American Motors 313

RAMBLER
You'll make the Smart Switch for '56

Product of American Motors

AMERICAN MOTORS MEANS *More for Americans*

See Disneyland—great TV for all the family over ABC network.

YOU SAVE ON FIRST COST. Model for model, Rambler is lowest-priced of all, with similar equipment, yet you get luxuries that rival the $5,000 cars—Power Brakes standard on custom models!

YOU SAVE 1/3 ON GASOLINE. New Typhoon OHV engine, with 33% more power, delivers up to 200 more miles on a tankful than other low-price cars.

DE LUXE 5615

SUPER 5618-1

$2230 — America's lowest-priced 4-door station wagon, delivered at the factory, including federal taxes. State and local taxes (if any), white wall tires and optional equipment (if desired), extra.

new 120-HP SIX with OVERHEAD VALVES

79,166 BLT.

new BROADER GRILLE ENCOMPASSES HEADLIGHTS

56 (RESTYLED) 108" WB ON ALL

Box-Girders All Around Passengers — Box-Sections Absorb Impact — SEE THE DIFFERENCE — The Old Way

Make the Smart Switch to Double Safe Single Unit Car Construction. All-welded, twice as rigid with "double lifetime" durability—means higher resale value.

NOTE VARIATIONS IN UPPER SIDE TRIM

CUSTOM

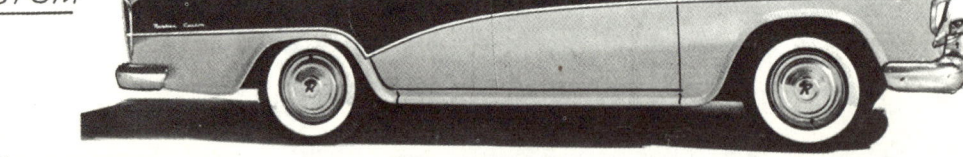

Make the Smart Switch to the car that out-corners, out-parks them all. Entirely new ride—first low-priced car with Deep Coil Springs on all four wheels.

"Make the Smart Switch to Rambler!"

new COLOR SPEAR SIDE MOULDINGS ON CUSTOM

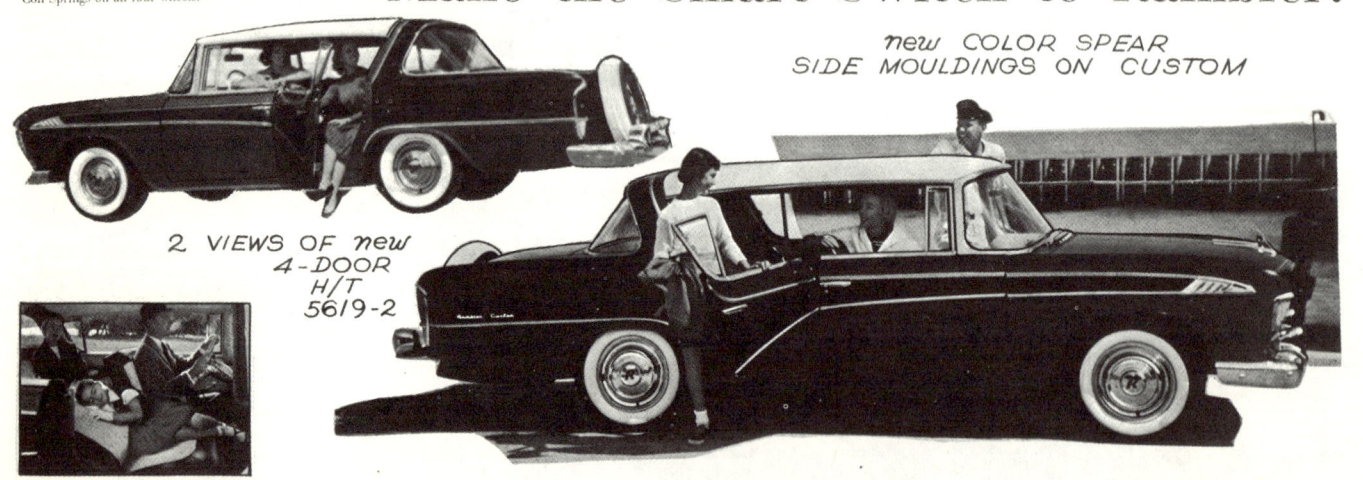

2 VIEWS OF new 4-DOOR H/T 5619-2

Make the Smart Switch to Airliner Reclining Seat luxury. You have a nap couch to keep children fidget-free on trips, relax grown-ups. Even a chaise longue!

new ROLL-DOWN REAR DOOR WINDOW 5618-2

FLASH! RAMBLER TOPS MOBILGAS ECONOMY RUN FOR 2nd STRAIGHT YEAR! 24.35 m.p.g. with Hydro-Matic Drive!

New Rambler Cross Country Station Wagon! Enjoy more fun per mile and per dollar in America's lowest-priced four-door Custom Station Wagon.

314

OVERDRIVE AVAIL.

RAMBLER

CUSTOM

Rambler 6 or V·8

new **190 H.P. V·8 And Economy 6**

5718-1 (6)
5728-1 (V8)

5718-2 (6)
5728-2 (V8)
CROSS-COUNTRY

GEORGE ROMNEY PRESIDENT, AMERICAN MOTORS (UNTIL 2-62)

SUPER

new REBEL V8

5739-2

255 HP 327 CID V8

AVAIL. AS REGULAR OR HARDTOP WAGON

5723-2 (V8)

SIDE MOULDINGS CHANGED

57 20 MODELS

SMALL EXTRA PIECE ADDED, IN TOP SECTION OF GRILLE

114,084 RAMBLERS BLT. 1957

5729-2 (V8)

RAMBLER

5802 or 5806

DE LUXE

127 HP 6 SUPER

new AMERICAN 6 (100" WB) 42,196 SOLD

$1775., f.o.b. and up

58

new GRILLES

new TAIL-FINS (ON ALL BUT AMERICAN)

CUSTOM

MORE THAN 100 IMPROVEMENTS! 22 MODELS

INTRODUCED FOR 1958, new AMERICAN and AMBASSADOR MODELS have OWN GRILLES, DIFFERENT FROM THOSE OF OTHER RAMBLERS.

215-HP REBEL V8

REBEL V8

5829-2

DASH

5888-1 OR 2

new AMBASSADOR V8 117" WB
new = 4 HEADLIGHTS
270 HP (THROUGH '59)

$2822., f.o.b.

5889-2

186,227 RAMBLERS SOLD 1958

new "DEEP-DIP" RUSTPROOFING

316

RAMBLER

5902 5906   STATION WAGON

New 100 inch wheelbase Rambler American

AMERICAN

$1835 Suggested delivered price at Kenosha, Wisconsin, for 2-door sedan at left. State and local taxes, if any, automatic transmission and optional equipment, extra.

SUPER

5915-1

CUSTOM

5915-2

5904-1 AMERICAN WAGON is *new* 90 HP

PUSH-BUTTON TRANS. AVAIL.

REBEL 108" WB

CROSS-COUNTRY 5928-1 or 2

REBEL

5929-2 COUNTRY CLUB

AMBASSADOR

5985-1 or 2

117" WB   270 HP V8

AMBASSADOR CUSTOM

59

5989-2

DASH   317

$2822. f.o.b.

RAMBLER

AMERICAN

6005

90 HP

6004

DOORS NOW OPEN WIDER (75° INSTEAD OF 55°)

60

ROOF RACKS NOW ON ALL WAGONS

6002

$1781., f.o.b. and up

5015

6 DELUXE
108" WB
127 HP

6018 WAGON

SUPER
6015-1 (6)
6025-1 (V8)

SEDAN
6015-2 (6)
6025-2 (V8)

CUSTOM COUNTRY CLUB
6019-2 (6)
6029-2 (V8)

REAR DETAILS ↓

6018 OR 6028 (-2 OR 4)

CUSTOM
V8 = 200 HP

new REAR FENDERS

3 WIDE SEATS, 5 BIG DOORS. The tailgate is a fifth door with outside key lock so children can't open from inside. Rear seat passengers step in—no scrambling over seats or tailgate.

WAGON (6 OR 8-PASS.)
6088-1 TO 4

2881., f.o.b., and up

new "COMPOUND WRAP-AROUND" WINDSHIELD ON AMBASSADOR

434,704 RAMBLERS SOLD 1960

AMB. CUSTOM COUNTRY CLUB
6089-2

AMBASSADOR V-8
BY RAMBLER

318

The New Standard of Basic Excellence in Luxury Cars

RAMBLER

6104

6105

6108 4-DR. WAGONS also

AMER. PRICES START AT **1831.**, f.o.b. (6102)

6107-2 " -5

$2369., f.o.b., and up

All New! A Convertible

"THE NEW WORLD STANDARD OF BASIC EXCELLENCE"

AMERICAN 6
L-HEAD 90 OR 125 HP OHV

AMERICAN WAGON REAR DETAILS

new Ceramic-Armored Muffler

61 (RESTYLED)

CLASSIC 6 OR V8
127 OR 138 HP 6
OR
200 OR 215 HP V8

CLOSE DETAIL OF CLASSIC FRONT END

CLASSIC DELUXE

CLASSIC CUSTOM
6108-2 (6)
6120-4 (V8)
(CLASSIC 2 DR. WAGONS also)

...New! First acoustical ceiling of molded fiber glass

6188-1, 2 OR 4

AMBASSADOR V8
250 OR 270 HP

CUSTOM 400 SEDAN JOINS AMBASSADOR LINE

Rambler
World Standard of Compact Car Excellence

6185-5

319

RAMBLER '62

6206 — 90 HP 6

1962 RAMBLER AMERICAN DELUXE 4-DOOR SEDAN (Also offered in Custom series) **6205**

6208 — RAMBLER AMERICAN DELUXE 4-DOOR STATION WAGON (Also offered in Custom series)

1962 RAMBLER AMERICAN DELUXE 2-DOOR CLUB SEDAN Also offered in Custom and "400" series **6208**

RAMBLER AMERICAN "400" 4-DOOR STATION WAGON (Also offered in Deluxe and Custom series)

6207-5 AMERICAN "400" CVT.

new DOUBLE SAFETY BRAKES with TANDEM MASTER CYLINDER

6216-2 new
1962 RAMBLER CLASSIC CUSTOM 2-DOOR CLUB SEDAN (Also offered in Deluxe and "400" series)

6215-5 CLASSIC 400

6218-5 RAMBLER CLASSIC 6 "400" CROSS COUNTRY STATION WAGON

454,784 RAMBLERS BLT. 1962

1962 RAMBLER AMBASSADOR CUSTOM 4-DOOR STATION WAGON **6288-2**

WB CUT TO 108"
250 OR 270 HP AMB. V8s
AMBASSADOR 400 AND INTERIOR

6285-5

RAMBLER

TOP QUALITY AT AMERICA'S LOWEST PRICE! **$1846**
Manufacturer's suggested retail price for the '63 Rambler American "220" Two-Door Sedan. Optional equipment, transportation, and state and local taxes, if any, extra. An award-winning Rambler value!

6302 ← 220

6304 220 →

6309-7
440-H H/T
(with 138-HP OHV 6)

6305
AMERICAN 6
100" WB

440 CVT.
6307-5

6306-5 440

63
(CLASSICS and AMB. TOTALLY RESTYLED)

DASH

6315-2
660

CLASSIC
6 or V8
new 112" WB

OPTIONAL 198-HP V8 (STARTING 3-1-63)

770
6315-5

770
6318-5

The New Shape Of Quality

New! Hidden storage compartment in wagon!

250 or 270 HP
AMBASSADOR V8
new 112" WB

880 CROSS COUNTRY
6388-2
990 WAGON SIMILAR

New! Curved glass side windows ... far easier entry!

6386-5
2-DR.

990

AMBASSADOR has LOWER BODY BAND

6385-5
SEDAN

321

WINNER OF MOTOR TREND AWARD
CAR OF THE YEAR

RAMBLER
new AMER. WAGON RESEMBLES A SEDAN with GRAFTED-ON REAR SECTION
330
220
6.00 x 14 TIRES (15" OPT.)
6406
220
6408
6405-2
6407-5
AMERICAN
440-H
6409-7
TOP IN BLK., WHITE, GOLD OR TURQ.
440
TO 138 HP
AMERICAN
TOTALLY RESTYLED (new 106" WB)
6418-5
6418
770
660
2-DR.
550
CLASSIC
(6 has 127 OR 138 HP)
64
6416-2
770
4-DR.
6415-5
393,863 RAMBLERS BLT. 1964
6489-5
990-H (INTERIOR BELOW)
6488-5
FRESH NEW SPIRIT OF '64!
DASH (W/O AIR CONDITIONING)
990
DASH (WITH AIR CONDITIONING)
990
250 OR 270 HP
AMBASSADOR

RAMBLER

6506 220

6508-2 6509-7 American 440-H

AMERICAN 330 American 6

New! 3 different sizes of cars
New! 3 different wheelbases
New! 7 spectacular powerplants:
New Torque Command Sixes—
most advanced engines! Big V-8's

L-HEAD 195.6 CID 6 STILL AVAIL. IN AMERICAN (90 HP @ 3000 RPM)

65

CVTS. NOW IN ALL 3 LINES

6507-5

DASH (AMERICAN)
112,736 RAMBLERS SOLD 1965

AMERICAN GRILLE NOW VERTICALLY SPLIT INTO 4 HORIZ. SECTIONS

440

195.6 OR 232 CID OHV 6s with 125 OR 155 HP

6517-5 6518-5 Rambler Classic 770 Station Wagon

770

CLASSIC

199 OR 232 CID 6 (128, 145, 155 HP)
198 HP with 287 CID V8

6519-5 Rambler Classic 770 Hardtop

SEE ALSO: MARLIN

CLASSIC DASH
770 SEDAN

GRILLE CLOSE-UPS

CLAS.

ALSO AVAIL. with 327 CID, 270-HP V8 ALSO USED IN AMB.)

AMB. (NEW HEADLIGHTS VERTICALLY STACKED)

CLASSIC 112" WB CONT'D., BUT AMBASSADOR WB INCREASED TO 116".

6515-5

6587-5

6589-7

AMBASSADOR V8

990

DASH

AMBASSADOR 1965

SLOGAN: **THE SENSIBLE SPECTACULARS**

RIVIERA (by Buick)

(STARTS 1963)

401 CID V8
325 HP @ 4400 RPM

117" WB

7.10 x 15 TIRES

(DASH)

63 America's bid for a great new international classic car

64

'64 DASH

ADVENTURE IS A CAR CALLED RIVIERA — AND IT'S A BUICK

(VINYL TOP ALSO AVAIL.)

new TAIL-LIGHTS IN BUMPER

65 new CONCEALED HEADLIGHTS

WIRE WHEEL OPTION →

Wouldn't you really rather have a Buick?

324

STUDEBAKER

(CARS = 1902-1966)

STUDEBAKER CORP., SOUTH BEND, IND.

$660. up (CHAMP.)

116½" WB (SINCE '38)

COMMANDER 6
226.2 CID
90 HP @ 3400 RPM

CLUB SEDAN

40

CHAMP. 6 has 164.3 CID
78 HP @ 4000 RPM

CHAMP. 2-DR. IS PACE CAR AT 1940 INDY 500 RACE.

250.4 CID   122" WB
PRESIDENT 8
110 HP @ 3600 RPM

→ 110" WB

Lowest priced CHAMPION

new WIDER GRILLES

You seldom use the clutch!
That's due to Studebaker's famous gas-saving, engine-saving Economatic Shift with Overdrive — available on all Champion models at moderate extra cost.

PRICES BEGIN AT $690
for a Champion Business Coupe
Champion Club Sedan with trunk .. $730
Champion Cruising Sedan with trunk .. $770

new 169.6 CID, 80 HP (CHAMP.)

COMMANDER
94 HP @ 3600 RPM

119" WB

41

new BAND TAPERS ALONG SIDES (EXCEPT ON SKYWAY)

Distinctively smart, new SKYWAY PRESIDENT 8

Land Cruiser
AVAILABLE ON COMMANDER SIX OR PRESIDENT EIGHT CHASSIS

117 HP @ 4000 RPM
125" WB

STUDEBAKER

CHAMPION 6 has 170 CID (SINCE '41 and THROUGH '54)

HIGHEST QUALITY CAR IN LOWEST PRICE FIELD

4-G
Champion 6

PRICES BEGIN AT **$810*** for a Champion Business Coupe

110" WB
5.50 × 16 TIRES

42-45

119" WB
6.25 × 16 TIRES

12-A
The Commander 6

Studebaker is building an unlimited quantity of airplane engines, military trucks and other matériel for national defense ... and a limited number of passenger cars which are the finest Studebakers ever produced.
— *The Studebaker Corporation*

CHAMPION ... $810 and up
COMMANDER ... $1108 and up
PRESIDENT 8 ... $1242 and up
f.o.b.

Skyway **COMMANDER** LAND CRUISER 6

PRESIDENT IS FINAL STRAIGHT-8
(FIRST PRES. 8 was 1928 MODEL)
124½" WB

8-C

World's first cars with Studebaker's new, perfected
Turbo-matic Drive
NO CLUTCH-PEDAL NO CREEP NO CLASH
Fluid coupling — with controlled gear selection — and automatic overdrive — available on President and Commander models at extra cost.

The President 8

OVERDRIVE AVAIL.

SKYWAY CHAMPION IS ONLY SERIES AVAIL.

"DOUBLE DATER" COUPE

DASH

EARLY **46**

RARE!
(AVAIL. ONLY TO MAY, '46)

$916.. f.o.b.

110" WB

326

BODIES AVAIL. — 3-PASS. COUPE;
5-PASS. "DOUBLE DATER" CPE.;
2-DR. CLUB SED.; 4-DR. CR. SEDAN

ALL-NEW 1947 MODELS START MAY, 1946

$1447.

First by far with a postwar car!
THE NEW 1947 STUDEBAKER
$1442. f.o.b.

new 112" WB ON 6-G CHAMPION

47 (TOTALLY RESTYLED)

Starlight COUPES

CHAMPION STRLT. CPE. (ABOVE) has 1-PC. WINDSHIELD, UNLIKE OTHER CHAMPION MODELS

$1752.

(SAME HP FIGS. SINCE '41) 14-A COMMANDER 119" WB

SEDAN

COMMANDER REGAL DE LUXE

DETAILS OF 2-DOOR SEDAN (CHAMP. REGAL DE LUXE)

$1910.

REGAL DE LUXE LAND CRUISER

123" WB

CONVERTIBLE (new)

CHAMPION 3 W. CPE.

new HORIZONTAL PIECE ACROSS EITHER END OF CHAMPION GRILLE

$1535., f.o.b.

New 1948 Studebaker
First in style

CHAMPION

SEDANS

$2077. COMMANDER

48

new HORIZ. CHROME ABOVE CMNDR. GRILLE

327

"First in style...first in vision...first by far with a postwar car"

$1762

CHAMPION (8-G)
NOW has 2 HORIZ. STRIPS ACROSS GRILLE

$1757.

$2135., f.o.b.

VERTICAL CHROME CENTER STRIP ADDED TO CMNDR. GRILLE

STARLIGHT CPE. and INTERIOR

STUDE. "STARLIGHT" CLUB COUPES ARE AMONG THE MOST UNUSUAL and ATTRACTIVE BODY STYLES EVER PRODUCED!

49

LAND CRUISER INTERIOR

REAR

lowest price

new 113" WB (CHAMPIONS)   85 HP

50

new "BULLET-NOSE" FRONT END STYLING

CHAMPION CUSTOM 6-PASS. 2-DOOR SEDAN AS SHOWN

$1487.50

the "next look" in cars   new 6.40 x 15 TIRES   (CONT'D.)

$1676.

CHAMPION
REGAL
DE LUXE 6

CHROME ALONG
ROCKER PANEL

Studebaker

50
(CONT'D.)

2-DR.
$1566.
CHAMPION DLX. (9-G)
has RUBBER PAD ON REAR FENDER,
BUT NO CHROME ALONG ROCKER PANEL.

CVT.

America likes Studebaker's new driving thrill—Every 1950 Studebaker handles with light-touch ease—rides so smoothly it almost completely abolishes travel fatigue. A new kind of coil spring front suspension.

COMMANDER (17-A)
$2024.
$2013.

LAND CRUISER
$2187.

America likes this "next look" in interiors —Fabulously fine nylon cord upholstery, introduced into motoring by Studebaker, is standard in the 1950 Land Cruiser and regal de luxe Commander. Land Cruiser is shown.

329

Studebaker Champion

CHAMP. CUSTOM HAS NO HOOD ORNAMENT

SEDAN

3-WINDOW BUSINESS COUPE
$1643.

51

232.6 CID IN new O.H.V. V8 ENGINE ALSO AVAIL.

CHAMPION DE LUXE 6 (10-G) 85 HP

$1744.
(REGAL CHAMP. has LEATHER TRIM INSIDE DOORS.)

A brand new V-8 (233 CID) *Commander* CVT.

has **120 h.p.** @ 4000 (THROUGH '54)

STATE CMNDR. SEDAN
$2143.

"BULLET NOSE" GRILLE SOMEWHAT MODIFIED FROM '50. new GRILLE IS FLUSH WITH FRONT END

COMMANDER LAND CRUISER
$2289.

330 "STUDEBAKER...THE THRIFTY ONE FOR '51"

STUDEBAKER'S 100TH ANNIVERSARY
1852-1952

© 1952, The Studebaker Corporation
South Bend 27, Indiana, U.S.A.

CHAMPION PRICES START AT $1735.

REGAL COMMANDER

REGAL CHAMPION OR STATE COMMANDER CONVERTS. AVAIL.

PACE CAR AT 1952 INDY 500 RACE

LAND CRUISER

52 FRONT END RESTYLED

BODY DESIGN BASICALLY AS BEFORE, BUT CONTROVERSIAL "BULLET NOSE" DISCONTINUED IN FAVOR OF A MORE CONVENTIONAL (BUT EXTREMELY BROAD) GRILLE

"STARLINER" H/T is new

* EDITED PHOTO (FROM AD) CAUSES THE WOMAN DRIVER TO APPEAR UNUSUALLY SMALL, IN COMPARISON TO CAR.

STATE COMMANDER

* = A TRICK TO MAKE CAR APPEAR LARGER

See and drive the **Studebaker Starliner**—It's America's smartest "hard-top"—available either as a Champion or a Commander V-8.

Studebaker

Awarded to Studebaker-1953

↑ new DESIGN WINS FASHION ACADEMY AWARD

53 (TOTALLY RESTYLED)

H/T

CHAMPION PRICES START AT $1735.

85 HP @ 4000 RPM

170 CID 6 (THROUGH '54)

← MEANS CHAMP. 6 H/T

new 116½" WB (120½" ON CPE., H/T and LAND CRUISER)

↑ MEANS CMNDR. V8

NO MORE CONVERTIBLES AVAILABLE (UNTIL '60 LARK)

VERTICAL PIECES ADDED TO GRILLE for 1954.

STUDEBAKERS, SINCE LATE 1930s, ARE Styled by *Raymond Loewy* →

CHAMPION PRICES START AT $1758.

54

CHAMPION CUSTOM

6 CYL. has 101 HP @ 4000 RPM (new 186 CID THROUGH '58)

A BIG NEW CHAMPION
America's No. 1 economy car!
Now more marvelous than ever!

CHAMPION PRICES START AT $1741.

CHAMPION DE LUXE

55

COUPES COMMANDER

INTERIOR (CMNDR.)

Now in the low price field!
A sensationally high-powered
NEW COMMANDER V-8

SPEEDSTER

(6-CYL. OR V8 WAGONS)

CONESTOGA

STATE PRESIDENT

COMMANDER H/T DETAILS

NEW!
AMERICA'S SMARTEST TWO-TONING!

PRESIDENT

The first dynamic headliners of the great Studebaker-Packard alliance! Sensationally powered '55 Studebakers! Amazingly low introductory prices!

224 OR
new 259 CID
V8s have
140, 162,
175 OR 185 HP

333

CHAMPION PRICES START AT
$1841.
Studebaker
Craftsmanship with a Flair
PELHAM 6
CHAMPION 6
wagons
PARKVIEW V8
FLIGHT HAWK 6
CMNDR. V8
POWER HAWK V8
SKY HAWK V8
FRONT DETAILS OF COMMANDER V8
NEW DUAL EXHAUSTS• Built into the bumper for more style, more class than you've ever seen in a low price car. Ready for 4-barrel carburetion to boost mileage and power.
Hawks
The Golden Hawk
GOLDEN HAWK V8 (275 HP)
56
SEDAN
PRESIDENT V8
CLASSIC SEDAN has ROCKER PANEL TRIM
"CLASSIC" SEDAN
259, 289 OR 352 CID V8s
PRESIDENT V8 195 HP * @ 4500 RPM
new 12-VOLT ELECTRICAL SYSTEM
NEW CYCLOPS-EYE SPEEDOMETER
* 210 HP with 4-BBL. CARB.
PRESIDENT PINEHURST V8

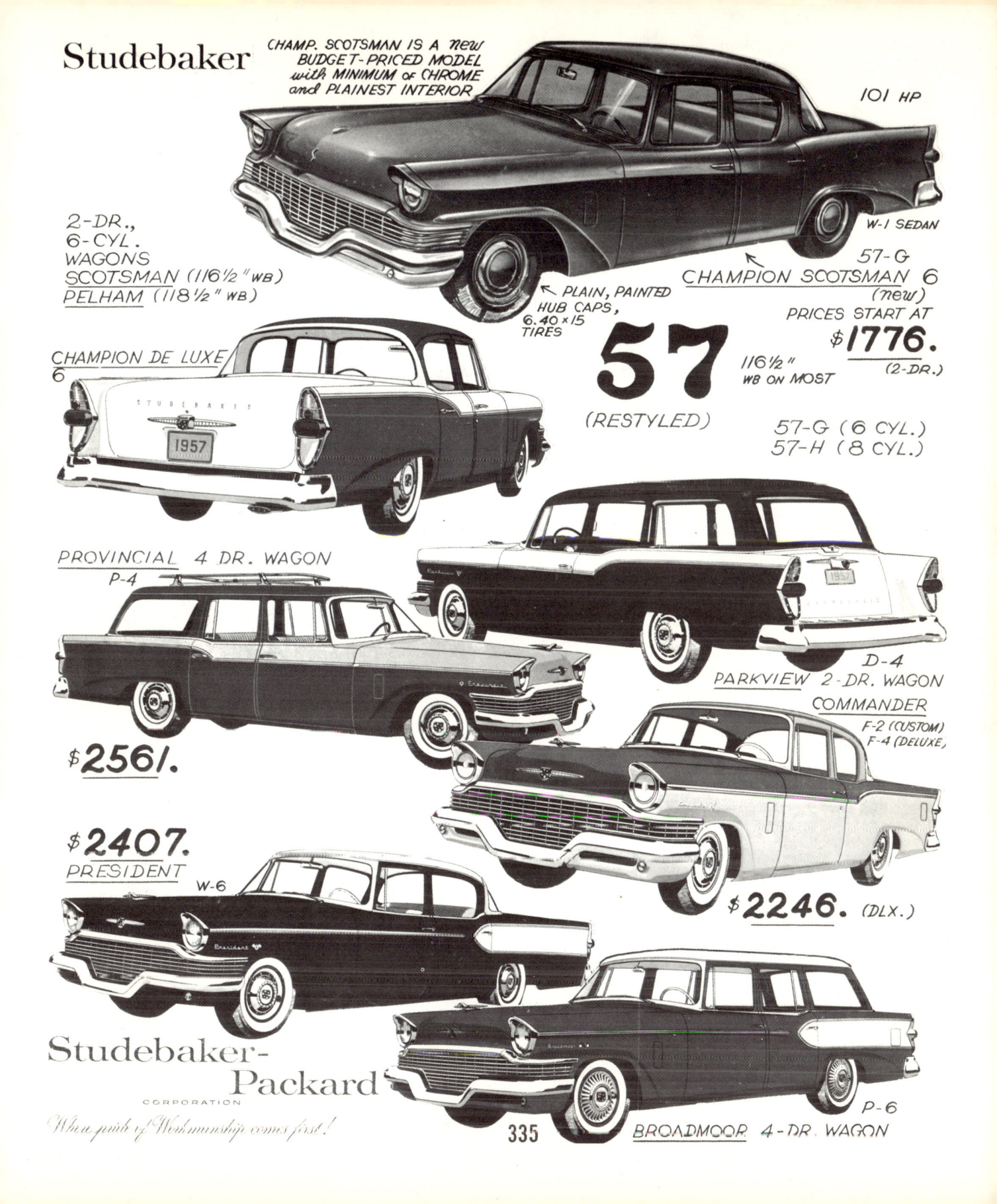

Studebaker

CHAMP. SCOTSMAN IS A NEW BUDGET-PRICED MODEL with MINIMUM of CHROME and PLAINEST INTERIOR

101 HP

2-DR., 6-CYL. WAGONS
SCOTSMAN (116½" WB)
PELHAM (118½" WB)

W-1 SEDAN
57-G CHAMPION SCOTSMAN 6 (new)
PRICES START AT $1776. (2-DR.)

← PLAIN, PAINTED HUB CAPS, 6.40 x 15 TIRES

57 (RESTYLED)

116½" WB ON MOST

57-G (6 CYL.)
57-H (8 CYL.)

CHAMPION DE LUXE 6

PROVINCIAL 4 DR. WAGON P-4

$2561.

D-4 PARKVIEW 2-DR. WAGON

COMMANDER
F-2 (CUSTOM)
F-4 (DELUXE)

$2407. PRESIDENT W-6

$2246. (DLX.)

Studebaker-Packard
CORPORATION

When pride of Workmanship comes first!

335

BROADMOOR 4-DR. WAGON P-6

289 CID (275 HP @ 4800 RPM)
V8 GOLDEN HAWK

C-3 SILVER HAWK
186 CID 6 (101 HP)

K-7

$3185.

57 (CONT'D.)

OR 210, 225 HP V8s (289 CID)

Golden Hawk

Studebaker Commanders and Champions

58

4 HEADLIGHTS ON SOME MODELS

101 TO 275 HP

(SAME HP AS '57) THE FINAL GOLDEN HAWK

180-HP CMNDR.

"Studebaker cars take on a completely new luxury look for 1958!"

SCOTSMAN 6 PRICES START AT $1795.

NOTICE STRIKING DIFFERENCES IN APPEARANCE BETWEEN THE LT.-OVER-DK. AND DK.-OVER-LT. HARDTOPS

REAR DETAILS (SEDAN)
Studebaker President

The Hawk-inspired PRESIDENT STARLIGHT for 1958

Studebaker-Packard CORPORATION
Where pride of Workmanship comes first!

336

STUDEBAKER

59
HAWK 6 PRICES START AT $2360.

6 OR V8
SILVER HAWK (C-6)

170 CID 6 (90 HP @ 4000) OR 259 CID V8s (180 OR 195 HP @ 4500)

SEE ALSO: **LARK** (STARTING 1959, LOWER-PRICED MODELS USE LARK NAME)

1959
120 ½" WB

60
3 new STRIPS on SIDE of REAR FENDER

new 289 CID V8 RETURNS TO HAWK AS ONLY AVAIL. ENG. (210 OR 225 HP @ 4500 RPM)

$2650.

C-6 HAWK
6.70 x 15 TIRES

61
new TRIM DESIGN ALONG REAR FENDERS

HAWK

$2677.
(C-6)

62 (RESTYLED)
new HAWK GT
new ROOFLINE
new CLASSIC-STYLE GRILLE with HEAVY CHROME BORDERS

$3424. (UP $27. IN '63)
(K-6)

63
new GRILLE DESIGN with DECORATIVE CRISS-CROSS STRIPS ADDED

HAWK GT

new AVANTI

AVANTI INTRO. DURING '62 109" WB
$4759. 289 CID V8

337

STUDEBAKER

6.00, 6.50 OR 6.70 × 15 TIRES

AVANTI V8

113" WB

109" WB

64

109" WB COMMANDER

CHALLENGER (109" WB)
(AVAIL. 1964 ONLY)
112 HP 6 OR 180 HP V8

$2417.

113" WB ON CRUISER V8

120" WB

FINAL GRAN TURISMO HAWK

STUDE. PRODUCTION CONTINUES ONLY AT THE CANADIAN BRANCH FACTORY, FOR '65-66.

DETAILS OF WAGONAIRE ILLUSTR. AT RIGHT

TOPSIDE LUGGAGE RACK (OPT.)

BRAKE RELEASE

Wagonaire

65

6 CYL. OHV ENG. (V8 ON NEXT PG.)
COMMANDER

"*the Common-Sense Car*"

TAILGATE STEP

(UNFOLDS AND LOWERS)

INTERIOR

338

$2581. (6 CYL.)

(CONT'D.)

Studebaker
THE COMMON-SENSE CAR

65 (CONT'D.)

Daytona Sports SEDAN

CRUISER INTERIOR FEATURES

Exclusive Beauty Vanity in glove compartment—(opt.).

CLOSER DETAIL OF DASH

DAYTONA INTER.

V8 NOW has 195 HP

← FINAL YEAR of 4 HEADLIGHTS

$2985.

Cruiser

S = 6
V = V8

PRICES START AT $2465. (COMMANDER 6 2-DR.)

194 cid, 120-HP 6 or 283 cid, 195-HP V8

FINAL STUDEBAKERS HAVE THIS GRILLE.

Studebaker AUTOMOTIVE SALES CORPORATION

LAST

Cars BY ST.-P.

66

109" or 113" WB (SINCE 1962, ON LARK and LARK-BASED MODELS)

339

3-66 = DISCONTINUED

TEMPEST BY PONTIAC!

new COMPACT CAR

NEW 4-CYL. ENG. ADAPTED FROM THE RIGHT HALF OF A PONTIAC V8!

FROM $2329.

new FOR **61**

STD. and CUSTOM COUPES INTRO. IN MIDYEAR

4 (STD.) (194.5 CID)
OR
V-8 (215 CID)

Independent suspension at all wheels

112" wheelbase (THROUGH '63)

THE HOT TOPIC IS THE NEW TEMPEST BY PONTIAC

TROPHY 4 ENGINE

FOUR CYLINDERS

to **155 h.p.** (Or buy the 155 h.p. aluminum V-8 option.)

FRONT ENGINE ⟷ REAR TRANSMISSION
PERFECT BALANCE

PONTIAC'S TEMPEST
PICKED BY MOTOR TREND MAGAZINE AS
CAR OF THE YEAR

WITH
340 PONTIAC POWER STEERING (OPT.)

TEMPEST

62

STANDARD TEMPEST COUPE has BROAD BACKLIGHT, MINIMUM CHROME

CUSTOM COUPE has "TOWN CAR" BACKLIGHT

4 CYL. WITH 110, 115, 120, 140, OR 166 HP. 185-HP ALUMINUM V8 ALSO AVAIL.

new LE MANS

The gas-saving "4" with Pontiac Punch!

LE MANS

4 CYL. 195.4 CID (115-166 HP) TEMPEST (NAME RETURNS TO FRONT FENDER)

CVT. WITH TOP DOWN

LE MANS

326 CID V8 ALSO AVAILABLE (260 HP)

LE MANS WITH TOP UP

LE MANS has RECTANGULAR TAIL- LIGHTS, "LE MANS" ON FRONT FENDER.

63

Wide-Track Pontiac Tempest

341

64 (RESTYLED)

Tempest
new 115" WB
new 215 CID
140-HP IN-LINE
O.H.V. 6

SAFARI WAGON

Tempest CUSTOM

326 CID V8 ALSO AVAIL.
(250 OR 280 HP)

LE MANS

LE MANS

GTO ("GTO" APPEARS ON GRILLE) (new)

1964

342

TEMPEST

1965: The year of the Quick Wide-Tracks

SAFARI WAGON

TEMPEST

Tempest

FROM $2618.

65

140-HP 6
OR
250-285 HP V8

TEMPEST CUSTOM

H/T (new)

Le Mans

FRONT-END COMPARISON OF LE MANS (left) and GTO (right)

SEE ALSO: **Pontiac**

OFFICIAL PACE CAR · MOTOR TREND RIVERSIDE "500" COURTESY OF HURST

GTO

343

THUNDERBIRD (Ford)

(INTRO. FALL, 1954, FOR 1955)

ALL with V-8 O.H.V. ENGINES

193 HP

102" WB (THROUGH '57)

6.70 x 15 TIRES (THROUGH '56)

(MODEL 40) **55** "CLASSIC" T-BIRDS AVAIL. with REMOVABLE HARD TOP OR CVT. TOP (THROUGH '57)

$2944.

56 40-B H/T has new PORTHOLES (EXCEPT EARLY MODELS)

40-A

202 HP

new 7.50 x 14 TIRES

57 GRILLE, BUMPERS, TAIL-LIGHTS MODIFIED

NAME MOVED TO FRONT FENDERS

212 HP

$3408.

new WHEEL COVERS

new DASH

344

THUNDERBIRD

58 (TOTALLY RESTYLED)

DASH 63-A

Exclusive "Panel Console"
new 113" WB
76-A

300 HP (THROUGH '65)

The car everyone would love to own!

CVT. 76-A

H/T 63-A

new 8.00 × 14 TIRES

HORIZONTAL PCS. ON GRILLE and BETWEEN TAIL-LIGHTS

59

new SIDE TRIM EACH YEAR

9 VERTICAL CHROME BANDS on EA. REAR FENDER (1960 ONLY)

6 TAIL-LIGHTS in 1960

$4222.

new GRILLE

60

sliding sun roof (new)

'60 THUNDERBIRD
THE WORLD'S MOST WANTED CAR

345

'61 THUNDERBIRD
UNIQUE IN ALL THE WORLD

$ 4637.

PACE CAR AT 1961 INDY 500 RACE

(OPTIONAL)

Swing-Away Steering Wheel glides out of your way for easier, more graceful entrances and exits—yet locks safely in place before you can drive.

61 (TOTALLY RESTYLED)

$4170.

unmistakably New, unmistakably Thunderbird

new BODY TYPES and MODEL NUMBERS in 1962

HARDTOP

CVT.

LANDAU (new)

$5552.

$4511.

with VINYL TOP and DECORATIVE LANDAU IRONS

Thunderbird Sports Roadster (new)

new GRILLE

62

new SPTS. RDST. has TWIN TONNEAU CAPS (as illustrated)

H/Ts = MODEL 83
CVTS. = MODEL 85

346

unique in all the world

THUNDERBIRD

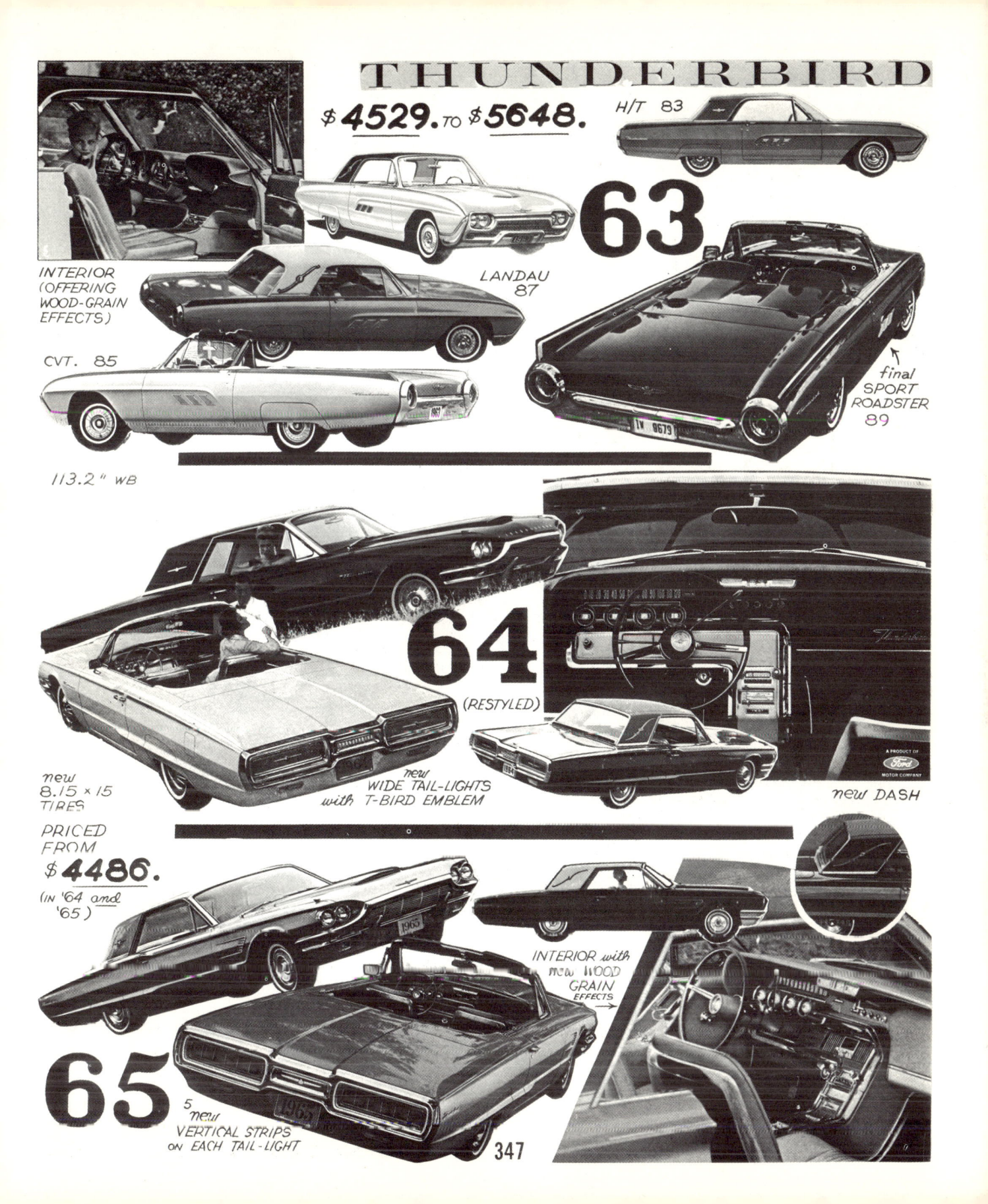

$4529. to $5648.

H/T 83

63

INTERIOR (OFFERING WOOD-GRAIN EFFECTS)

LANDAU 87

CVT. 85

final SPORT ROADSTER 89

113.2" WB

64 (RESTYLED)

new 8.15 x 15 TIRES

new WIDE TAIL-LIGHTS with T-BIRD EMBLEM

new DASH

PRICED FROM **$4486.** (in '64 and '65)

65 5 new VERTICAL STRIPS on EACH TAIL-LIGHT

INTERIOR with new WOOD GRAIN EFFECTS

347

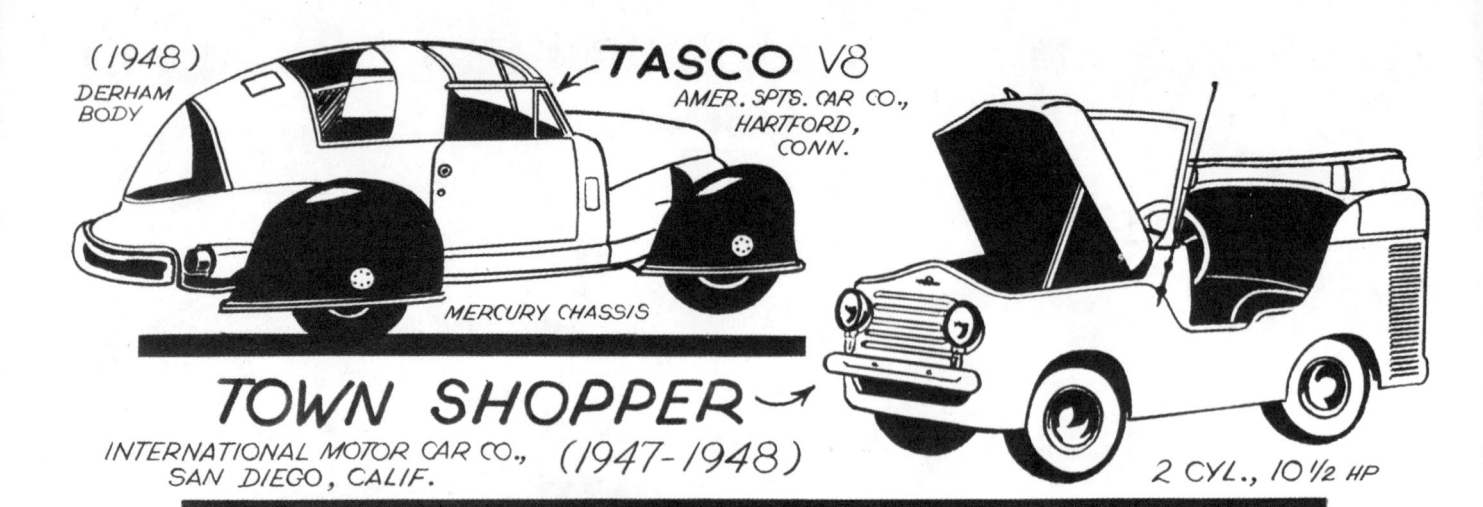

(1948) **TASCO** V8
DERHAM BODY
AMER. SPTS. CAR CO., HARTFORD, CONN.

MERCURY CHASSIS

TOWN SHOPPER (1947-1948)
INTERNATIONAL MOTOR CAR CO., SAN DIEGO, CALIF.

2 CYL., 10½ HP

Tucker '48
THE TUCKER CORP., 7401 S. CICERO, CHICAGO, ILL. (1946-1949)

PRINCIPAL OUTPUT PRODUCED DURING 1947, BUT KNOWN AS 1948 MODELS.

PRESTON TUCKER (FOUNDER) (1903-1956)

6-CYL. HORIZ. OPPOSED FRANKLIN/TUCKER REAR ENGINE

TURNING (CENTER) "CYCLOPS EYE" HEADLIGHT

CRASH COWL

RARE! ONLY 53 BUILT, INCLUDING PILOT MODELS.

SYMBOL OF SAFETY

348

Valiant NEW FROM CHRYSLER

V-100

$2053. and up

V-200

V-200s have EXTRA SIDE CHROME TRIM.

INCLINED 6-CYL. 170 CID O.H.V. ENGINE 101 HP @ 4400 RPM or 148 HP @ 5200 RPM

V-200

106½" WB (THROUGH '62)

1960

60 QX1-L OR QX1-H

V-100

225 CID PLYMOUTH 6 CYL. ENGINE ALSO AVAIL. (145 HP @ 4000 RPM)

V-200

new H/T

V-200

DASH

V-200

note GRILLE CHANGE

FINAL YEAR FOR 148-HP VERSION OF SMALL ENGINE

61 RV1-L OR RV1-H

V 200

349

VALIANT

$2590.

V-100

V-200

62

SVI

SVI-L (V-100)
SVI-H (V-200)
SVI-P (SIGNET)

new SIGNET (has FRONT BUCKET SEATS)

$2538.

↑ SIGNET has ▽ INSIGNIA ON DARK GRILLE

(new 18-GALLON FUEL TANK)

Valiant V-100 2-door sedan/metallic green

ENGINE

new CONVT.

TRANSMISSION PUSHBUTTONS

106" WB

63 TVI

(TOTALLY RESTYLED)

Valiant V-200 4-door station wagon/dark metallic blue

350

VALIANT

note THAT THIS LATER SERIES CONVERTIBLE has LESS REAR BRIGHTWORK and DIFFERENT DECK EMBLEM FROM "SIGNET" ILLUSTR. on PRECEDING PAGE

63 (CONT'D.)

Valiant presents
AMERICA'S LOWEST-PRICED CONVERTIBLE...$2340*

Barracuda (new) (INTRO. 4-2-64)

$2215. — V-100

Valiant V-100 2-Door Sedan

6 CYL. or V8

64

V-200

$2670. (6)

VV1-L (V-100)
VV1-H (V-200)
VV1-P (SIGNET 200)
VV1-P29 (BARRACUDA)

new 273 CID V8 has 180 HP @ 4200 RPM

$2549.

SIGNET

new GRILLE with "PLYMOUTH" NAMEPLATE ABOVE

Valiant/64 style
Best all-around compact

$2766.

351

VALIANT

BARRACUDA

$2801. (V8)

65

6 and V8 ENGINE SPECS. AS BEFORE, EXCEPT THAT new OPTIONAL 10.5 COMPRESSION VERSION OF V8 IS ALSO AVAIL., with 235 HP @ 5200 RPM

ALL-VINYL SEATS IN "100."

100

Plymouth Valiant 200 4-Door Station Wagon

6 CYL.:
AV1-L (100)
AV1-H (200)
AV1-P (SIGNET)
AV1-P29 (BARRACUDA)
(V8s have "AV2" PREFIXES)

200

200

The Roaring '65s*

DASH

Valiant Signet

new FLAT-PROFILE AIR CONDITIONER

$2234. TO $2932.

352   *= SLOGAN APPLIES TO PLYMOUTH ALSO.

COUPE

(WILLYS NAME SINCE 1917)
(ALSO WILLYS-KNIGHT, OVERLAND, WHIPPET)

WILLYS

WILLYS-OVERLAND
MOTORS, INC.
TOLEDO, O.
PRICED FROM $495.

DE LUXE

4 CYL. ONLY (SINCE '34 and THROUGH '47)

40 "4-40"

FLAT-BACKED
LOWER-PRICED "Speedway" MODEL DOES NOT HAVE THE EXTRA STRIPS (HORIZONTAL) ALONG FRONT END OF HOOD.

102" WB
4.3 GEAR RATIO

new = REAR QUARTER WINDOWS (SEDAN)

RED-LETTERED "AMERICAR" NAME ON HOOD STRIP

new 1-PC. VERTICAL-BARS GRILLE ON '41.

41 "4-41"

new 104" WB

new PLAINSMAN MODELS (AT TOP OF LINE) OFFER OVERDRIVE and ALUMINUM HI-COMPR. CYL. HEAD AS STD. EQUIP.

new 4.4 GEAR RATIO

AMERICAR

new BISECTED GRILLE

FROM $695.

42 "4-442"

ALSO

Jeep

(SEE FOLLOWING PAGES)

353

WILLYS 'Jeep' Station Wagon

UNIVERSAL JEEP (4-W-D)

MILITARY STYLE ('46)

$1146.

EARLY MODEL ('46)

All-Steel Station Wagon (new) ENGINE

MILITARY JEEPS INTRO. '41

46-47
CJ-2A SERIES

('47)

$1565.

"Jeep Station Wagon" ON HOOD

104" WB

new 6-CYL STATION SEDAN

has IMITATION WICKER PANELS

(PHOTOGRAPHED IN PORTLAND, ORE.)

4 CYL. (6 CYL. IN STA. SED.)

48

JEEP LT. TRUCKS ALSO AVAIL.

EXPORT MODEL (note PLAIN BUMPER SOMETIMES USED)

(CONT'D.)

354

WILLYS 48 (CONT'D.)

the Jeepster $1765.

JEEPSTER CVT. PRODUCED TO 1953; RE-INTRO. BY KAISER-JEEP, 1967.

4 or 6 CYL.

New

JEEPSTER $1595. (FOR 4 CYL.)

THE 'Jeep' Station Wagon

6-CYL. ENGINE NOW AVAIL. ALSO IN WAGON or JEEPSTER. 4-CYL. ALSO CONTINUES. 63 HP

49

'Jeep' Station Sedan
6 CYL. only

DEEP UPHOLSTERED SEATS, interior roominess and road-leveling wheel suspension add to the smooth, luxurious riding comfort of the 'Jeep' Station Sedan.

$1890.

355

WILLYS 'Jeep'

('50)

JEEPSTER

('51)

new GRILLE (EARLY '50 has '49-STYLE GRILLE.)

50-51

MILITARY JEEP

FIRST NON-JEEP WILLYS CAR PRODUCED SINCE 1942 MODELS:

The Revolutionary New Aero Willys

108" WB

AERO-WING ('52 ONLY)

AERO-ACE

52

AERO-LARK has 6-CYL. L-HEAD engine; WING, ACE, EAGLE have HURRICANE 6 F-HEAD. JEEP WAGONS, JEEPSTERS also

DETAILS OF F-HEAD COMBUSTION CHAMBER

New Hurricane 6 Engine, F-head design with 7.6 compression, one of the world's most efficient power plants.

356

Willys Aero

FIFTIETH YEAR ANNIVERSARY OF WILLYS-OVERLAND 53

AERO LARK

NO HOOD ORNAMENT ON LARK

2-DR.

AERO-LARK DELUXE →

AERO-ACE

4-DR.

AERO-FALCON (REPLACES '52 AERO-WING) (AERO-FALCON 2-DR RESEMBLES LARK DLX.)

AERO-ACE 2-DR.

ACE H/T ALSO AVAIL. (ILLUSTR. AT LOWER RIGHT)

AERO-EAGLE H/T

AERO ACE H/T →

Station Wagon

JEEP 4 (4-W-D)

JEEP 6 DELUXE

Willys Aero

AERO FALCON NO LONGER AVAIL.

← REAR SPARE TIRE

AERO EAGLE CUSTOM

LARK, ACE, EAGLE MODELS

54
K-W
Kaiser-Willys Sales Div.
Willys Motors, Inc.

H.P. INCREASED

90 OR 115 HP

WAGON has new GRILLE

WIDER OPENING TOP DOOR GIVES WIDEST OPENING OF ANY STATION WAGON IN ITS FIELD

CUSTOM   4 OR 6 CYL.

4-W-D

all-new GRILLE, TAIL-LIGHTS and TRIM

55

BERMUDA H/T

FINAL WILLYS CARS BUILT IN U.S.A., BUT JEEP PRODUCTION CONTINUES. KAISER JEEPS BLT. 1963 TO 1969. AMERICAN MOTORS CORP. BEGAN BUILDING JEEPS (SINCE START OF 1970 MODEL SEASON.)

Automotive library additions

The Cobra Story. Autobiography of Carroll Shelby and Cobra production & racing history through 1965. 288 pages, 61 photos.

Make Money Owning Your Car. Down-to-earth analysis on beating the high depreciation and interest costs of car ownership. 179 pages, 96 photos.

Hudson: The Postwar Years. In-depth analysis of Hudson models and the company's demise; much information never before published. Well illustrated, 136 pages.

Chrysler & Imperial: The Postwar Years. Fascinating story of this innovative and engineering-oriented marque. 216 pages, 469 photos and illustrations.

American Car Spotter's Guide 1920-1939. Illustrates models of 217 U.S. makes. 290 pages, 2,607 pictures, softbound.

The Specification Book for U.S. Cars 1920-1929. Important features of more than 400 makes of American passenger cars. 325 pages, softbound.

The Lincoln Continental. Photos, history and technical information through 1961. 210 pages, 202 illustrations, softbound.

Buick: The Postwar Years. The comprehensive history of one of America's styling and engineering leaders. Well illustrated.

The Production Figure Book For U.S. Cars. The only authoritative source for U.S. car production information. Truly reflects the relative rarity of various makes, models, body styles, etc. Softbound, 180 pages.

Shelby's Wildlife: The Cobras and Mustangs. Complete, exciting story of the 260, 289, 427 and Daytona Cobras plus chapters detailing the Shelby Mustangs. 224 pages, nearly 200 photos.

American Truck Spotter's Guide 1920-1970. An identification guide showing 170 makes of U.S. truck models with more than 2,000 illustrations. Softbound, 336 pages.

Motorbooks International
Publishers & Wholesalers Inc
Osceola, Wisconsin 54020, USA